TAPAS

• FOODS OF THE WORLD •

TAPAS

RICHARD TAPPER
Photography by Joyce Oudkerk Pool

LITTLE BROWN
AND COMPANY
BOSTON • TORONTO • LONDON

A Little, Brown book

A Lansdowne Production
Level 5, 70 George Street, Sydney NSW 2000, Australia

© Copyright Lansdowne Publishing Pty Ltd, Australia, 1993
© Copyright design: Lansdowne Publishing Pty Ltd, Australia, 1993

This edition first published in 1994

ISBN: 0-316-90607-7
A CIP catalogue record for this book
is available from the British Library

Food stylist: Daniel Bowe
Designed using Quark Express in 10/11 Garamond and Avant Garde
Printed in Singapore by Kyodo Printing (S'pore) Pte Ltd

Little, Brown and Company (UK) Ltd
165 Great Dover Street
London SE1 4YA

CONTENTS

INTRODUCTION

To the average Spaniard the local tapas bar provides the three things held dearest—good food, good wine and the opportunity to offer an opinion in convivial conversation. Much of Spain's social and business conversation is held in cafes and bars, and no one would dream of a drink without *algo para picar*—something to nibble at; in other words, tapas. The word *tapa* literally means "lid", and the origin of the tapas custom most probably lies in the placing of a small plate or lid over a glass of wine when served. It is also said that a centuries-old decree insisted that all bars and roadhouses must serve food as an accompaniment to wine, in an attempt to ensure at least a modicum of sobriety among the nation's coach drivers.

Whatever its origins may have been, the daily gathering before lunch or dinner for the ritual partaking of tapas, as both an appetizer and an adjunct to conversation, is now an integral part of the Spanish way of life. Tapas have evolved into an almost separate style of cuisine.

Some areas of Spain, such as the waterfront barrios of Barcelona, seem to contain little else but tapas bars, each offering their own specialty. Some serve half a dozen dishes, some as many as seventy or eighty. Whether it be Barcelona or the *tascas* of Madrid or any other Spanish city or town, the bars will be individualized by the origins of their proprietors. It is almost impossible to go anywhere in Spain without encountering both Basque and Galician tapas bars boasting a rich offering of seafood and shellfish dishes. Who could forget his first encounter with *Pulpo a la Gallega* (Octopus Galician Style) or any one of the dozens of clam and mussel dishes, not to mention the myriad ways of preparing squid and the smell of shrimp (prawns) grilling in garlic and olive oil on the *plancha* (griddle). It is these seafood dishes from the Bay of Biscay states that are the most easily adaptable abroad, but this is not to say that we should ever overlook the Moorish-influenced dishes of the south, like *Pinchos Morunos* (Moorish-style Kebabs), or the rich heritage of the peninsula's interior, which offers the flavor of a real Spanish omelet along with meat, game, poultry, beans, chickpeas and hundreds of different sausages and pies. The Mediterranean coast and the Balearic Islands also offer an incredible variety of seafood and meat dishes.

Bars also advertise themselves according to the conversational predilections of their patrons, whether it be discussing *jai alai*, the bullfight, football, the arts or politics. Running a tapas bar seems to be a noble form of retirement for past sporting heroes.

Tapas are a tradition long peculiar to Spain, but in the last two decades we have seen their emergence from the peninsula to the United States, particularly New York and California, where the proliferation of tapas bars and their popularity are testament to the public's willingness to embrace the notion of a more sensible social style of drinking. The latter part of the 1980s saw the concept become truly international, and we have seen the launching of several highly successful tapas establishments in Australian cities and the rising popularity of tapas as a form of entertaining. The idea and style of tapas remain quintessentially Spanish but it is a theory and cuisine that lends itself easily to adaptation.

In this book a large number of the recipes are authentically Spanish, but I have not allowed myself to become too restricted by tradition; there are even overtones of Asian influence. This reflects my own experiences, since as well as having owned and operated a tapas bar for six of the ten years I lived in Spain, I have also spent several years in India and Southeast Asia.

Nevertheless, whenever I prepare and serve tapas it is with a Spanish classical guitar tape playing. The food is served in Spanish crockery and there is always an attempt to somehow reproduce the slightly eccentric conviviality of an authentic Spanish tapas bar.

Buen provecho!

Note for the American reader:

Throughout this book, the word PRAWN refers to SHRIMP. For each recipe where shrimps are used, a guide is given as to size, which is referred to as 'small', 'medium' or 'large'. The recipes are suitable for all species of shrimp, and the type chosen depends on availability and the cook's individual tastes.

MARINATED OLIVES
Aceitunas Aliñadas

The secret of marinating your own olives is to leave them marinating as long as possible—a minimum of three weeks and a maximum of six months.

Green Olives
8 oz/250 g canned or loose green olives with their stones. Drain off any liquid and lightly crush the olives. Add 12 peeled and crushed large garlic cloves and 1 tablespoon chopped fennel. Put in a sealable glass jar and top up with olive oil. Cover and store in the refrigerator for a few weeks, turning occasionally. Serve at room temperature.

Black Olives
8 oz/250 g unpitted black olives, drained and lightly crushed. Add 2 to 12 crushed and peeled garlic cloves, according to taste, and 1 or 2 dried red chilies. Top up with red wine vinegar and a dash of lemon juice. Keep in a sealed jar at room temperature for a minimum of 3 weeks.

Piquant Olives
Remove the stones from 8 oz/250 g large green olives and thread a green chili through each. Pickle for a minimum of 3 weeks in a solution of white wine vinegar and a dash of lemon juice. These are a favorite in many Spanish tapas bars and are great appetizers with predinner drinks.

STUFFED ARTICHOKES
Alcachofas Rellenas
8 tapas servings

8 artichokes
olive oil
½ cup/2 oz/60 g minced onion
8 oz/250 g ground (minced) lean pork
3 oz/100 g ground (minced) ham
½ cup/2 oz/60 g breadcrumbs
2 tablespoons chopped parsley
salt and freshly ground black pepper
Zesty Tomato Sauce (page 11)

1. Trim the top ¾ to 1¼ in (2 to 3 cm) off the artichokes and boil in salted water until tender.

2. In a pan heat about 1 tablespoon olive oil and fry the onion, pork and ham together until the pork is barely cooked. Remove from heat and drain off any excess fat. Add the breadcrumbs, parsley, salt and pepper, and mix well.

3. Push down on each artichoke so that the outer leaves splay out and the choke is exposed. Remove the choke, then fill artichoke with the stuffing.

4. Preheat oven to 350°F/180°C/Gas 4. Cut the stalk from each artichoke in such a way that the artichoke will stand upright. Arrange in a baking pan. Sprinkle with a little olive oil and bake for 20 minutes. Serve hot with Zesty Tomato Sauce.

STUFFED ARTICHOKES II
Alcachofas Rellenas II
8 tapas servings

8 medium artichokes
2 tablespoons white wine vinegar
3 tablespoons Spanish olive oil
½ cup/2 oz/60 g finely diced onion
1 ½ teaspoons each minced ginger and minced garlic
1 tablespoon flour
½ cup/4 fl oz/125 ml tomato puree
1 large red bell pepper (capsicum), roasted whole, skin and seeds
removed, pureed (page 19)
1 tablespoon butter
1 lb/500 g raw shrimp (prawns), peeled and chopped
salt and freshly ground black pepper
1 tablespoon cognac
2 eggs, lightly beaten
½ cup/2 oz/60 g breadcrumbs
1 large red bell pepper (capsicum), seeded and finely diced
grated Parmesan cheese (optional), Zesty Tomato Sauce (page 11)

1. Trim top ¾ in (2 cm) off artichokes. Boil until tender in salted water with the vinegar (do not overcook). Refresh in cold water.

2. In a pan heat half the olive oil and fry the onion, ginger and garlic for 2 to 3 minutes. Stir in the flour and cook for 1 minute, stirring constantly. Add the tomato and pepper puree and simmer for 10 minutes.

3. Melt the butter in another pan over medium heat. Add the shrimp and cook only until they have changed color. Refresh in cold water.

4. Season the tomato mixture. Add the cognac and cook 5 minutes, then let cool. Add egg, breadcrumbs, diced pepper and shrimp.

5. Push down on each artichoke so that the outer leaves splay out and the choke is exposed. Remove the choke, being sure to leave the base intact. Fill artichokes with shrimp stuffing.

6. Preheat oven to 475°F/250°C/Gas 9. Cut stalk from each artichoke in such a way that it will stand upright. Arrange in a baking pan. Sprinkle with remaining olive oil and bake for 10 to 15 minutes. If desired, sprinkle with Parmesan cheese about 5 minutes before removing the artichokes from the oven. Serve hot with Zesty Tomato Sauce.

ZESTY TOMATO SAUCE

This sauce is a delicious accompaniment to stuffed artichokes.

olive oil
1 onion, finely chopped
3 garlic cloves, finely chopped or pressed
16 oz/465 g can Italian tomatoes
1 red chili, seeded and chopped
2 bay leaves
salt and freshly ground black pepper

Heat a little olive oil in a pan and fry the onion and garlic until transparent. Add the tomatoes, chili, bay leaves, salt and pepper and cook until reduced to a good sauce consistency, 20 to 30 minutes.

SPANISH FLAG
Bandera Español
12 to 15 tapas servings

This is not a genuine *tapa* but the dish I invariably use as a centerpiece when serving an array of tapas. The red and yellow bell peppers (capsicums) used in this dish closely resemble the colors of the Spanish flag. It looks best on an oval platter about 18 inches (45 centimetres) long.

6 red and 6 yellow bell peppers (capsicum), roasted and cut into
3 × 2 in/7.5 × 5 cm rectangles (page 19)
10 oz/300 g salami, thinly sliced
10 oz/300 g *chorizo*, thinly sliced
7 oz/200 g black olives
7 oz/200 g green olives
1 lb/500 g artichoke hearts

Arrange the bell peppers around the rim of the platter, overlapping and alternating the red and yellow colors all the way around. Arrange the salami slices around inside the pepper strips, overlapping slightly to cover any untidy ends, then a ring of *chorizo*, a ring of black olives, where the salami and *chorizo* meet, and a ring of green olives inside the *chorizo*. The artichoke hearts go in the center.

FRIED EGGPLANT (AUBERGINE) WITH PARMESAN CHEESE
Berenjenas con Queso
8 tapas servings

You may want to keep one batch of the eggplant warm in the oven while you work on the next, but if left too long this will go soggy.

2 medium eggplants (aubergines)
2 eggs
4 garlic cloves, minced
2 cups/16 fl oz/500 ml water
1 cup/8 fl oz/250 ml olive oil
flour
7 oz/200 g Parmesan cheese, finely grated

1. Cut the eggplants crosswise into ⅓ in (1 cm) slices. Mix the eggs, garlic and water.

2. Heat the olive oil to medium hot in a pan. Meanwhile, dredge the pieces of eggplant in flour, coat with egg mixture and then dip into the cheese, making sure both sides are coated. Fry in the oil for about 2 minutes on each side or until golden brown. Drain on paper towels. Serve immediately.

STUFFED EGGPLANT (AUBERGINE)
Berenjenas Rellenas
8 tapas servings

4 small to medium eggplants (aubergines)
¼ cup/2 fl oz/60 ml Spanish olive oil
1 large onion, finely chopped
6 garlic cloves, finely chopped
1 celery stalk, finely chopped
1 red bell pepper (capsicum), seeded and finely chopped
1½ tablespoons self-raising flour
1 cup/4 oz/125 g fresh breadcrumbs
2 egg whites, beaten
salt and freshly ground pepper
2 tablespoons freshly grated Parmesan cheese
basil sprigs (garnish)
herbed tomato sauce*

1. To make the sauce*, finely chop 2 large onions, 4 cloves garlic and 1½ teaspoons ginger and fry in 1 tablespoon olive oil for 3 minutes. Add 1 lb/500 g fresh tomatoes (1 lb/465 g can) and cook for 10 minutes over medium heat. Puree, then add the basil and coriander. Measure 1 cup/8 fl oz/250 ml of the sauce, setting aside the remainder.

2. Preheat oven to 475°F/250°C/Gas 9. Cut the eggplant in half lengthwise and deeply score the flesh in a crisscross pattern, being careful not to cut the skin. Use 2 tablespoons oil to coat the flesh then place the eggplants on a baking sheet and bake for 8 to 10 minutes or until almost cooked. Scoop out flesh, leaving a thickness of ⅓ in (1 cm) still attached to the skin. Puree flesh in a food processor and set aside.

3. Fry onion and garlic in 1 tablespoon olive oil for 3 minutes. Add celery and bell pepper and cook a further 3 minutes. Add the reserved tomato sauce and eggplant puree and cook for 5 minutes. Remove from heat and stir in flour and breadcrumbs. Let cool for 10 minutes, then fold in the egg whites. Season with salt and pepper.

4. Stuff the eggplants with the mixture and place in a baking dish that has been brushed with the remaining tablespoon of olive oil. Cover half of each stuffed eggplant with the Parmesan cheese. Bake for 10 to 15 minutes or until nicely browned. Spoon remaining sauce over the other half of each eggplant and garnish with basil sprigs.

14

MUSHROOMS WITH BACON
Champiñones con Tocino
6 *tapas servings*

1 tablespoon olive oil
4 oz/250 g diced *tocino* or bacon
2 garlic cloves, finely chopped or pressed
1 lb/500 g button mushrooms
½ cup/4 fl oz/120 ml dry white wine
salt
2 teaspoons freshly ground pepper
1 tablespoon chopped parsley

Heat the olive oil in a pan and fry the *tocino* over high heat for 3 minutes. Add the garlic and mushrooms and stir well. Add the wine, salt, pepper and parsley and cook over high heat for 3 to 4 minutes or until most of the wine has evaporated and the mushrooms are cooked. Serve hot.

MUSHROOMS IN GARLIC AND PARSLEY
Champiñones al Ajillo
6 tapas servings

6 garlic cloves, finely chopped or pressed
¼ cup/2 fl oz/60 ml olive oil
1 lb/500 g mushrooms
2 tablespoons chopped parsley
1 tablespoon flour
1 cup/8 fl oz/250 ml water
salt and freshly ground pepper
juice of ½ lemon

1. Fry the garlic in the olive oil for 1 to 2 minutes, making sure it doesn't burn. Add the mushrooms and parsley and simmer until the mushrooms begin to exude liquid.

2. Add the flour and stir until the liquid becomes a paste, then stir in the water, salt, pepper and lemon juice. Simmer for 10 minutes, adding a little more water if the sauce is too thick. Serve hot.

STUFFED MUSHROOMS
Champiñones Rellenos
8 tapas servings

¼ cup/2 fl oz/60 ml olive oil
1½ teaspoons finely chopped garlic
32 2 in (5 cm) size button mushrooms, stalks removed
1 tablespoon finely chopped onion
¼ cup/1 oz/30 g minced *tocino* or bacon
1 tablespoon finely chopped parsley
1 egg, lightly beaten
2 tablespoons fresh breadcrumbs
2 tablespoons grated Parmesan cheese

1. Heat the olive oil and garlic in a pan large enough to hold all the mushrooms. Add the mushrooms, tops down, and sauté gently for about 2 minutes or until browned but not cooked through. Remove the mushrooms.

2. Add the onion and *tocino* to the pan and sauté for 2 to 3 minutes. Pour off any excess liquid. Add the parsley and remove from heat; let cool.

3. Add the egg and breadcrumbs and mix well. Stuff the mushroom caps with the mixture and top each one with Parmesan cheese. Broil (grill) or bake in a hot oven until the cheese has browned and the mushrooms are cooked through. Serve at once.

WHITE BEANS WITH BLOOD SAUSAGE
Judías Blancas con Morcilla
6 to 8 tapas servings

Another famous Spanish staple is garbanzos (chickpeas), which can be substituted for the white beans in this recipe. This dish improves in flavor if cooked the day before and reheated.

8 oz/250 g dried white beans, soaked overnight
2 oz/50 g salt pork, diced
2 bay leaves
olive oil
1 onion, finely chopped
3 garlic cloves, finely chopped
2 oz/50 g blood sausage, chopped
1 tablespoon chopped parsley
1 ½ teaspoons flour
freshly ground pepper
1 ½ tablespoons anise liqueur such as ouzo or Pernod

1. Drain the beans, rinse and cover generously with fresh water. Bring to boil. Remove from heat and let stand 30 minutes.

2. Change the water and bring the beans to boil again, adding the salt pork and bay leaves. Cook for 1 hour.

3. Drain off excess water so that the beans are barely covered. Return to low heat. In a separate pan, heat 2 tablespoons olive oil and fry the onion and garlic until transparent. Add the blood sausage and parsley and fry for 2 minutes. Stir in the flour and pepper and cook for 1 minute. Pour in a little water from the beans and stir to a sauce consistency. Drain the beans and add to the pan (save some of the cooking liquid in case the sauce needs diluting).

4. Cook the mixture over low heat for 1 hour or until the beans are tender. Stir in the liqueur and cook for 5 more minutes.

ROASTED PEPPERS (CAPSICUMS)
Pimientos Asados
6 tapas servings

Roasted peppers are commonly used on their own, as an integral part of many other dishes and as a garnish. If you are serving them whole as a tapa, it is best to use smaller peppers. When used as an ingredient or garnish, the peppers are invariably cut into thin strips or very finely diced. They make an excellent addition to chicken or seafood salads. For a separate dish you will need six red bell peppers (capsicums).

1. Brush the peppers with a little olive oil and bake in a medium to hot (350 to 400°F/180 to 200°C/Gas 4 to 6) oven for about 30 minutes, or roast on a barbecue or griddle (hot plate) for a shorter time; the peppers are cooked as soon as they collapse.

2. Peel and seed the peppers and place in a bowl. Toss with a dressing of olive oil, a little lemon juice and salt and pepper. If you wish, add a bit of anchovy, chopped onion and parsley.

POTATO SALAD
Ensaladilla
8 tapas servings

This common mayonnaise-and-potato salad will be found in every tapas bar in Spain and is invariably one of the first dishes to be presented each day. It begins as a highly decorated mound of salad on a large platter and diminishes as the day progresses.

6 potatoes, boiled, peeled and diced
½ cup/2 oz/60 g diced cooked carrot
½ cup/2 oz/60 g cooked green peas
salt and freshly ground pepper
1 cup/8 fl oz/250 ml garlic mayonnaise (page 114)
1 red and 1 green bell pepper (capsicum), roasted, skinned, seeded and cut into strips (page 19)
parsley sprigs

Mix the potatoes, carrot, peas, salt, pepper and mayonnaise. Mound on a platter and garnish with the red and green pepper strips and the parsley. The flavor will improve if the salad is left standing for an hour or more at room temperature.

POTATOES IN SPICY SAUCE
Patatas Bravas
8 tapas servings

5 tablespoons olive oil
8 large potatoes, peeled and cut into 1½ in (4 cm) cubes
1 large onion, finely chopped
3 garlic cloves, finely chopped
2 tablespoons finely chopped parsley
3 fresh chilies, chopped and seeded, or 1 tablespoon *sambal oelek*
(page 115)
2 cups/16 fl oz/500 ml pureed canned Italian tomatoes
½ cup/4 fl oz/125 ml dry white wine
salt
chorizo or chopped bacon (optional)

1. Heat four tablespoons olive oil in a pan until smoking; add the potato cubes and brown thoroughly.

2. Preheat oven to 475°F/250°C/Gas 9. Transfer the potato and the oil to a baking dish and bake for about 15 minutes or until the potatoes are crisply cooked.

3. Meanwhile, heat the remaining tablespoon of olive oil in a pan and sauté the onion and garlic for 3 minutes. Add all remaining ingredients and simmer until the potatoes are cooked. Drain the potatoes and place in a serving bowl or individual dishes. Pour the sauce over them and toss; there should be just enough sauce to coat. Serve at once.

STUFFED RED PEPPERS
Pimientos Rellenos
6 to 8 tapas servings

In many traditional Spanish dishes the ingredients differ from household to household, bar to bar, restaurant to restaurant or region to region. It is possible to order a dish in ten different places and receive ten totally different things, even though all have the same name on the menu. *Pimientos Asados* (Roasted Peppers) is one such dish. Included here are the two versions that I found to be the most popular in Spain.

6 to 8 small red bell peppers (capsicums)
olive oil
½ cup/2 oz/60 g chopped onion
2 garlic cloves, finely chopped or pressed
1 small can (3 to 5 oz/100 to 150 g) tomatoes, finely chopped
2 red chilies, seeded and chopped
12 mussels, cooked and diced
1 small can (8 oz/250 g) whole clams, drained
1 tablespoon chopped parsley
salt and freshly ground pepper
½ cup/2 oz/60 g cooked white rice

1. Preheat oven to 400°F/200°C/Gas 6. Brush the whole peppers with a little olive oil and roast 15 minutes. Cut around the stalk of each pepper and pull it out; reserve. Remove the seeds.

2. Heat 2 tablespoons olive oil in a pan and sauté the onion and garlic until transparent. Add the tomato and chilies and cook until reduced to a smooth sauce. Add the mussels, clams, parsley, salt and pepper. Remove from heat and add the rice.

3. Preheat oven to 375°F/190°C/Gas 5. Stuff the peppers with the rice mixture, leaving room for it to expand. Replace the stalks. Arrange the peppers in a baking pan and brush with a little olive oil. Bake 10 to 15 minutes or until heated through. Serve hot.

STUFFED RED PEPPERS II
Pimientos Rellenos II
6 to 8 tapas servings

For an additional touch, serve *Pimientos Rellenos* with the Simple Tomato Sauce on page 97.

> 6 to 8 small red bell peppers (capsicums)
> 1 lb/500 g ground (minced) pork or lean beef
> 1 tablespoon olive oil
> ½ cup/2 oz/60 g finely chopped onion
> 3 garlic cloves, finely chopped or pressed
> 1 small can (3 to 5 oz/100 to 150 g) tomatoes
> 2 teaspoons chopped fresh rosemary
> 1 tablespoon chopped parsley
> salt and freshly ground pepper
> 6 green olives, very finely chopped
> 1 tablespoon sweet sherry
> 2 hard-boiled eggs, chopped

1. Prepare and roast the peppers as described in *Pimientos Rellenos* (page 22). Cook the meat in an ungreased pan, stirring frequently. Remove from the pan and drain well.

2. Add the olive oil to the pan and sauté the onion and garlic until transparent. Add the tomato, rosemary, parsley, salt and pepper and cook until reduced to sauce consistency. Stir in the meat and remove from heat. Stir in the olives, sherry and eggs.

3. Preheat oven to 375°F/190°C/Gas 5. Stuff the peppers with the mixture and replace the stalks. Bake 10 to 15 minutes or until heated through. Serve hot.

POTATO AND HAM CROQUETTES
Croquetas de Patata y Jamón
6 tapas servings

No Spanish tapas bar is complete without at least one variation of the ubiquitous *croquetas*. Whether they are made from ham, chicken, shrimp (prawns), fish, vegetables, meat or even rice, they invariably have one of two bases: mashed potatoes or a flour-and-milk dough that is crumbed and fried. Either way they are delicious. This first recipe is based on potato.

2 tablespoons butter
⅔ cup/3 oz/85 g ground (minced) ham
1 ½ teaspoons flour
½ cup/4 fl oz/125 ml milk
1 tablespoon chopped parsley
salt and freshly ground pepper
3 large boiled potatoes, mashed with no added ingredients
dash of lemon juice
flour for dredging
2 eggs, beaten with a little water
breadcrumbs
oil for frying

1. Melt the butter in a pan, making sure it doesn't burn. Add the ham and heat gently for 2 minutes. Stir in the flour and then the milk, parsley, salt (omit if the ham is salty) and pepper; cook for 1 minute. Stir in the mashed potato and finally the lemon juice.

2. If the mixture is too dry, add a little more milk, but take care not to add too much liquid. Let the mixture cool, then refrigerate for at least 1 ½ hours and up to 2 days.

3. Form the croquettes in a cylindrical shape 3 in (7.5 cm) long and 1 in (2.5 cm) in diameter and dredge in flour. Dip into the beaten eggs, then coat with crumbs. For best results, refrigerate the croquettes for at least 30 minutes.

4. Fry the croquettes in enough hot oil to cover, turning once. Drain on paper towels and serve immediately.

SEAFOOD CROQUETTES
Croquetas de Pescado
12 to 15 tapas servings

This second croquette recipe is based on a flour-and-milk dough.

7 tablespoons butter
1 cup/4 oz/125 g all purpose (plain) flour
1 cup/8 fl oz/250 ml milk
½ cup/4 fl oz/125 ml white wine
salt and freshly ground pepper
2 teaspoons hot paprika
10 oz/300 g boned cod or similar fish
3 oz/100 g shrimp (prawns), chopped
½ cup/1 oz/30 g chopped parsley
3 oz/100 g cooked mussels, finely chopped
flour for dredging
2 eggs, beaten with a little water
breadcrumbs
oil for frying

1. Melt the butter in a pan over low heat. Stir in the flour and cook for 2 to 3 minutes, stirring constantly; make sure the roux doesn't burn. Little by little whisk in the milk and wine. Add the salt, pepper and paprika and whisk until the mixture is completely smooth.

2. Stir in the fish, shrimp and parsley and cook for 5 minutes. Remove from heat and stir in the mussels. Let the mixture cool, then refrigerate 3 to 4 hours (or even better, overnight).

3. Shape the mixture into croquettes. Roll in flour, dip into the egg mixture and coat with crumbs. For best results, refrigerate for at least 30 minutes. Deep fry the croquettes in hot oil. (Fry one croquette as a test; if the oil is not hot enough the croquettes tend to disintegrate.) Drain on paper towels and serve immediately.

CHICKPEA CROQUETTES
Croquetas de Garbanzos
10 tapas servings

1 lb/500 g garbanzos (chickpeas), soaked overnight
1 onion, finely chopped
2 garlic cloves, finely chopped
1 egg, lightly beaten
2 teaspoons chopped parsley
2 teaspoons *sambal oelek* (page 115) or 2 teaspoons finely chopped chili
2 teaspoons cumin powder
2 teaspoons thyme
2 teaspoons salt
1 tablespoon lemon juice
2 tablespoons cornstarch (cornflour)
¼ cup/2 fl oz/60 ml olive oil
oil for frying

1. Boil the garbanzos until they are completely cooked, about 2 hours. In a separate pan, gently fry the onion and garlic in 2 tablespoons olive oil until the onion is transparent.

2. Mash or process in a blender together with the garbanzos and add all the other ingredients. The mixture should be dry enough to mold into small round croquettes 2 in/5 cm in diameter which are fried a few at a time in enough hot oil to cover them completely. These are excellent served hot with garlic mayonnaise (page 114) or with either of the sauces for empanadas (page 42).

VEGETABLE CROQUETTES
Croquetas de Verduras
10 to 12 tapas servings

14 oz/400 g can red kidney beans, drained
1 lb/500 g mashed potato, with no added ingredients
1 tablespoon finely chopped celery
1 tablespoon finely chopped onion
1 tablespoon finely chopped green (spring) onion
1 tablespoon finely chopped parsley
3 eggs
flour for dredging
3 tablespoons water
breadcrumbs
oil for frying

1. Puree the kidney beans in a food processor and mix thoroughly with the potatoes, celery, onions, parsley and 1 of the eggs. The mixture should be firm enough to shape into croquettes; if not, add enough breadcrumbs to bring it to the right consistency.

2. Shape mixture into cylindrical croquettes 3 in (7.5 cm) long and 1 in (2.5 cm) in diameter. Dredge in the flour, dip in an eggwash made from the remaining 2 eggs and the water, and then roll in the breadcrumbs. Deep fry in hot oil 350°F/180°C. Serve hot.

BATTER-FRIED VEGETABLES
Verduras Fritas
15 to 20 tapas servings

This popular tapas bar dish could be compared to tempura. (Not many people know that tempura did in fact originate on the Iberian peninsula, having been introduced to the Japanese by the Portuguese several hundred years ago.) In Spain, however, it is served with lemon wedges or garlic mayonnaise.

1 cup/4 oz/125 g all purpose (plain) flour
½ cup/2 oz/60 g cornstarch (cornflour)
1 cup/8 fl oz/250 ml cold water
1 eggplant (aubergine), thinly sliced crosswise
½ cauliflower, cut into small florets, blanched in boiling water for 3 to 4 minutes and drained
2 large onions, sliced into rings
2 zucchini (courgettes), cut into thin 2 in/5 cm strips
1 red or green bell pepper (capsicum), cut into 2 × ⅓ in/5 × 1 cm strips
seasoned flour for dredging
oil for frying
lemon wedges and/or garlic mayonnaise (page 114)

1. Using the flour, cornstarch and water, prepare a batter as in the recipe for *Pescado Frito* on page 88. Dredge the vegetable pieces in seasoned flour, shaking off excess.

2. Dip the vegetables into the batter and deep fry in oil heated to 350°F/180°C until golden brown. Drain on paper towels and serve immediately with lemon wedges and/or mayonnaise.

SERRANO HAM WITH ASPARAGUS
Jamón Serrano con Espárragos
8 *tapas servings*

Jamón serrano is a smoked ham which is usually served very thinly sliced. While its flavor is distinctly different from Italian prosciutto, the latter may be used as a substitute.

24 thin slices serrano
24 asparagus spears, trimmed and boiled for 1 to 2 minutes
(depending on thickness)
2 garlic cloves
½ cup/1 oz/30 g chopped basil
½ cup/8 fl oz/250 ml olive oil
1 tablespoon red wine vinegar
freshly ground pepper
finely diced red bell pepper (capsicum)

1. Wrap each asparagus spear in a slice of ham, leaving the tip protruding, and divide over 8 plates.

2. In a blender or food processor, blend the garlic, basil, olive oil and vinegar, and pour a little over each serve. Top with ground pepper and diced bell pepper.

MALLORCAN-STYLE SNAILS
Caracoles Mallorquinas
6 tapas servings

Prepare this dish with frozen, unseasoned snails. (Canned snails are usually available but do not have as much flavor.) Remember that snails should always be prepared in their shells and you shouldn't (for the purposes of this recipe) use any that have been seasoned in advance.

1 lb/500 g snails in their shells
olive oil
1 onion, finely chopped
5 garlic cloves, finely chopped or pressed
2 tomatoes, diced
3 oz/100 g diced salt pork
1 *chorizo* sausage, diced
½ cup/2 oz/60 g diced blood sausage
2 red chilies, seeded and chopped
1 ½ teaspoons flour
salt and freshly ground pepper
2 cups/16 fl oz/500 ml dry white wine
3 tablespoons anise liqueur (see note)
½ cup/1 oz/30 g chopped parsley
juice of 1 lemon

1. Wash the snails thoroughly. Heat about 2 tablespoons olive oil in a large pan and fry the onion and garlic until transparent. Add the tomato and simmer until cooked. Add the salt pork, *chorizo*, blood sausage and chili and cook for 2 to 3 minutes. Stir in the flour, salt and pepper and cook for 2 minutes.

2. Gradually stir in the wine and anise liqueur, then add the parsley and snails and simmer for 20 minutes. Add the lemon juice and simmer for another 15 minutes. Serve hot.

Note: In Mallorca they make a particular type of blood sausage that is flavored with anise. This is not available elsewhere, but ordinary blood sausage along with a nip of anise liqueur, such as ouzo or Pernod, makes a perfectly acceptable substitute.

CAMBOZOLA MARINATED IN TARRAGON AND GARLIC
Cambozola con Estragón y Ajo
8 tapas servings

Cambozola is an Italian cheese. You may prefer to use another tangy, firm-bodied white cheese, or a mixture of two or three of them.

You can easily vary this recipe according to taste, but be careful not to use ingredients that will totally overpower the cheese. I sometimes vary the herb or add two or three fresh or dried chilies to the marinade. Sun-dried tomatoes make a great accompaniment to this dish.

2 cups/16 fl oz/500 ml extra virgin olive oil
1 scant cup/7 fl oz/210 ml tarragon vinegar
2 tablespoons chopped fresh tarragon, or 2 teaspoons dried
2 teaspoons freshly ground pepper
1 head garlic, each clove smashed but unpeeled
1 lb/500 g Cambozola cheese, cut into ¾ in (2 cm) cubes
fresh tarragon sprigs and roasted red pepper (capsicum) strips
(page 19) for garnish

Combine the olive oil, vinegar, tarragon, pepper and garlic in an airtight jar and let stand for one week. Strain. Cover the cheese with the liquid and marinate for 2 days. Serve garnished with the tarragon sprigs and the pepper strips.

MALLORCAN PIZZA
Coca Mallorquín
12 tapas servings

Another version of *coca*, which was a special at my local *panadería* every Sunday morning, is topped with a mixture of spinach, tomato and sardines.

1 lb/500 g bread dough (I purchase pizza dough from my local pizzeria)
2 tablespoons olive oil
3 oz/200 g diced red bell pepper (capsicum)
3 oz/200 g diced green bell pepper (capsicum)
2 onions, thinly sliced
12 oz/350 g tomatoes, chopped
2 tablespoons chopped parsley
salt

1. Knead the dough on a board, adding the olive oil as you work it. Roll it out and line a shallow pan (about 13 × 9 in/35 × 20 cm) with the dough.

2. Preheat oven to 400°F/200°C/Gas 6. Mix the bell peppers, onion, tomato and parsley with a little salt and spread over the dough. Bake for 30 to 45 minutes or until the crust is golden brown.

OLIVE AND OVEN-DRIED TOMATO BREAD

Pan de Olivas y Tomates Secados

Makes 1 large loaf

This bread is best used the next day and is an excellent accompaniment to tapas.

⅓ oz/10 g fresh yeast
1 cup/8 fl oz/250 ml lukewarm water
14 oz/400 g all purpose (plain) flour
3 oz/100 g wholewheat (wholemeal) flour
½ cup/2 oz/60 g pitted and coarsely chopped sun-dried black olives
½ cup/2 oz/60 g Oven-dried Tomatoes (page 34)

1. Cream the yeast with 1 tablespoon water. Combine the flours and let warm in a low oven for 5 minutes, remove and add creamed yeast and ¾ of the remaining water. Mix well, adding more water if necessary, but remember the dough for this bread should be stiffer than normal dough. Knead well for about 10 minutes, until the dough develops a sheen. Shape dough into a round ball and place in a bowl of more than twice the volume of the dough. Cover bowl with a damp towel and leave in a warm place to rise.

2. When the dough has risen to double its volume, turn out, dust with flour and knead well for 5 minutes, constantly turning the dough in on itself. Shape into a ball, return to the bowl and allow to rise again to double volume.

3. Turn the dough out, add the olives and oven-dried tomatoes and knead for 3 to 4 minutes. Form dough into a round ball and place on a floured baking sheet. Invert the bowl over the dough and leave to stand until it has risen to double its volume. With a sharp knife gently make six intersecting cuts across the top of the dough. Stand for a few minutes more, allowing the cuts to open slightly. Meanwhile, preheat the oven to 450°F/230°C/Gas 8.

4. Bake on center shelf for 15 minutes, lower temperature to 400°F/200°C/Gas 6 and bake a further 15 minutes. Turn the oven off and leave the bread for 15 minutes before removing. Allow to cool completley before slicing.

OVEN-DRIED TOMATOES
Tomates Secados al Horno

Although sun-dried tomatoes are Italian in origin, they make an excellent companion to tapas, their flavor blending well with Spanish food. While they are available from most delicatessens, the flavor of the homemade variety is fresher and superior.

4½ lb/2 kg cherry tomatoes about 1 in (2.5 cm) in diameter, halved
24 garlic cloves, peeled
10 g finely chopped fresh thyme
sea salt
black pepper
40 fresh basil leaves
1 qt/1 l olive oil, plus

1. Lay the tomatoes out, cut side up, on drying racks that will fit in your oven (the mesh should be such that the air is able to circulate around the tomatoes and fine enough to prevent them from falling through as they shrink with dehydration). Intersperse the tomatoes with the garlic cloves and sprinkle with thyme, salt and pepper.

2. Place the drying racks over the racks in the oven. Bake at 300°F/150°C/Gas 2, with the door slightly open, for 6 to 7 hours, keeping an eye on the tomatoes. If they show signs of burning, lower the temperature. Remove from the oven before they are completely dried. Cool and set aside for immediate use, or preserve in sterilized jars mixed with the basil leaves and covered in olive oil.

SPINACH PASTRIES
Empanadas de Espinacas
8 to 10 tapas servings

1 tablespoon olive oil
2 garlic cloves, finely chopped
2 tablespoons finely diced *chorizo* or ham (optional)
1 large bunch spinach, stemmed, washed and chopped
1 red bell pepper (capsicum), roasted, peeled and seeded (page 19)
salt and freshly ground pepper
Empanada Pastry circles (page 111)
1 egg beaten with 2 teaspoons water

1. Heat the oil in a pan. Add the garlic and *chorizo* and fry for 1 minute. Add the spinach and toss until wilted. Add the red pepper and remove from heat. Let cool.

2. Squeeze out any liquid from the spinach mixture. Season with salt and pepper. Put 2 teaspoons of spinach mixture in the center of each pastry circle, remembering to take them from the refrigerator only four or five at a time. Fold them over and crimp the edges together. Refrigerate for at least 15 minutes.

3. Preheat oven to 475°F/250°C/Gas 9. Arrange the empanadas at least ¾ in (2 cm) apart on a greased baking sheet. Brush with egg wash. Bake for 5 to 6 minutes or until golden brown. Serve immediately.

FISH PASTRIES
Empanadas de Pescado
8 to 10 tapas servings

2 tablespoons olive oil
½ cup/2 oz/60 g finely chopped onion
2 garlic cloves, finely chopped or pressed
1 large tomato, chopped
1 red chili, seeded and chopped
salt and freshly ground pepper
1 tablespoon chopped parsley
1 tablespoon tomato paste (concentrate)
8 oz/250 g cooked and boned firm-fleshed fish such as tuna or cod
1 hard-boiled egg, chopped
1 red bell pepper (capsicum), roasted, peeled, seeded and diced
(page 19)
Empanada Pastry circles (page 111)
1 egg beaten with 2 teaspoons water

1. Heat the oil in a pan and fry the onion and garlic until transparent. Add the tomato, chili, salt and pepper and cook until somewhat thickened. Add the parsley and the tomato paste, diluted with a little water, and cook for 3 to 4 minutes. Remove from heat and let cool.

2. Mix the fish, egg and red pepper.

3. Assemble and bake the pastries as described in the Spinach Empanadas recipe on page 35.

KIDNEY VOL AU VENT
Pastel de Riñones
8 tapas servings

12 oz/350 g lambs' kidneys
flour
8 2½ in (6 cm) vol-au-vent cases
¼ cup/60 g/2 oz butter
1 onion, finely chopped
2½ cups/150 g/5 oz sliced mushrooms
2 teaspoons marjoram, finely chopped
freshly ground pepper
½ cup/4 fl oz/125 ml Spanish dry sherry
½ cup/4 fl oz/125 ml fresh cream

1. Clean the kidneys and slice as thinly as possible crosswise, discarding fat and sinew. Dust with flour. Preheat oven to 300°F/150°C/Gas 2 and warm the vol-au-vent cases.

2. In a pan, fry the onion in the butter until transparent, then add the kidneys, mushrooms, marjoram and pepper. Cook for 3 minutes then add the sherry and ignite. When the flame dies, add the cream and cook for a further 2 minutes, stirring continuously (the kidney slices should be cooked through). Spoon the mixture into the vol-au-vent cases and serve immediately.

OYSTER EMPANADAS
Empanadas de Ostras
8 to 10 tapas servings

48 oysters, shucked and finely chopped
1 scant tablespoon butter
1 tablespoon roux
4 green (spring) onions, very finely chopped, including green tops
½ cup/4 fl oz/125 ml heavy (thick) cream
1 tablespoon chopped parsley
freshly ground pepper
1 tablespoon Chinese oyster sauce or 1½ teaspoons Thai fish sauce
diced, sautéed bacon (optional)
Empanada Pastry circles (page 111)
1 egg beaten with 2 teaspoons water

1. Sauté the oysters gently in the butter. Stir in the roux and cook until thickened to a paste. Add all remaining ingredients and cook for about 3 minutes, allowing the mixture to thicken. Let cool.

2. Assemble and bake the pastries as described in the Spinach Empanadas recipe on page 35.

Roux: To make 1 tablespoon of roux melt ½ tablespoon butter in a pan. When it begins to foam whisk in 1 tablespoon flour. Reduce heat and allow paste to cook 1 minute.

CHICKEN LIVER EMPANADAS
Empanadas de Hígado de Pollo

8 to 10 tapas servings

1 onion, finely chopped
3 oz/100 g bacon, diced
1 tablespoon butter
10 oz/300 g chicken livers, chopped
2 tablespoons red wine
1 tablespoon cognac
2 teaspoons minced fresh sage
salt and freshly ground pepper
1 tablespoon roux (page 38)
Empanada Pastry circles (page 111)
1 egg beaten with 2 teaspoons water

1. Sauté the onion and bacon in butter for 3 minutes. Add the chicken livers and brown. Add the wine, cognac, sage and seasoning and cook until the livers are just cooked through. Stir in the roux and cook until the mixture is thickened. Let cool.

2. Assemble and bake the pastries as described in the Spinach Empanadas recipe on page 35.

SPICY SHRIMP AND SCALLOP EMPANADAS
Empanadas de Mariscos Picantes
8 to 10 tapas servings

8 oz/250 g peeled large shrimp (prawns), chopped
7 oz/200 g scallops, chopped
2 tablespoons butter
1 onion, finely chopped
2 garlic cloves, finely chopped
1 ½ teaspoons finely chopped fresh ginger
1 tablespoon hot Madras curry powder
1 tablespoon flour
½ cup/4 fl oz/125 ml canned unsweetened coconut milk
1 tablespoon chopped fresh coriander (cilantro)
salt (optional)
1 ½ teaspoons *sambal oelek* (page 115) (for a very spicy filling)
Empanada Pastry circles (page 111)
1 egg beaten with 2 teaspoons water

1. Gently sauté the shrimp and scallop meat in 1 tablespoon butter until they change color (they should not be cooked through). Tip them into a colander, refresh under cold running water and set aside.

2. In a pan melt the other tablespoon of butter and sauté the onion, garlic and ginger for about 3 minutes. Add the curry powder and flour and stir to make a roux; cook, stirring constantly, for 3 minutes. Add the coconut milk, coriander, salt and *sambal* and cook for 3 to 4 minutes, stirring to make sure the mixture is smooth. Add the shrimp and scallops and immediately remove from heat. Let the mixture cool.

3. Assemble and bake the pastries as described in the Spinach Empanadas recipe on page 35.

CHORIZO AND OLIVE EMPANADAS
Empanadas de Chorizo y Aceitunas
6 to 8 tapas servings

2 oz/60 g *chorizo*, finely chopped
1 oz/30 g pimento-stuffed green olives, finely chopped
1 tablespoon finely chopped red bell pepper (capsicum)
24 Empanada Pastry circles (page 111)

1. Mix the *chorizo*, olives and bell pepper together and place 1 to 2 teaspoons of the mixture on each pastry circle. Fold over and crimp the edges as described in the Empanada Pastry recipe. Place the empanadas in the refrigerator and let rest for 15 minutes.

2. Preheat oven to 475°F/250°C/Gas 9. Brush the empanadas with an egg wash made from 1 egg and 2 teaspoons water whisked together. Place the empanadas on a lightly greased baking sheet and bake for 5 minutes, or until they are golden brown and the pastry is cooked through. Serve immediately.

FAVORITE SAUCES FOR EMPANADAS

Although it is not traditional, I like the Indian method of serving *samosas*, Indian cousins to the empanada, with a sauce for dipping. Neither of these sauces is even vaguely related to Spanish cuisine, but they are the two I most often serve with empanadas—and I never serve tapas without empanadas.

CORIANDER CHUTNEY
Makes 2 cups/16 fl oz/500 ml

1 bunch fresh coriander (cilantro), roots included
3 green chilies, seeded
1½ cups/12 fl oz/375 ml unsweetened coconut milk, or plain yogurt
1 tablespoon chopped fresh ginger

Combine all ingredients in a blender or food processor and puree. Chill and serve or serve at room temperature.

SWEET CHILI SAUCE
Makes 3 cups/24 fl oz/750 ml

1 tablespoon *sambal oelek* (page 115)
1 tablespoon brown sugar
2 tablespoons granulated (white) sugar
3 cups/24 fl oz/750 ml white wine vinegar

Combine all ingredients in a nonaluminum pot and boil for about 10 minutes. Cool. This sauce will keep in the refrigerator for up to 3 months.

ANDALUSIAN BAKED EGGS
Huevos a la Flamenca
6 servings

As the name suggests, this dish has its origins in Andalusia, the southern province of Spain, which is home to a large proportion of the country's Gypsy population. *Huevos a la Flamenca* is popular throughout the peninsula. It is more of an entree or brunch dish than a *tapa*, but I include it because it is one of my favorites. I often vary this dish by adding a tablespoon of chili *sambal* (page 115) to the tomato mixture. You can also give it a sprinkling of Parmesan cheese, but don't overdo it.

1 onion, finely chopped
2 garlic cloves, finely chopped
2 tablespoons olive oil
1 lb/465 g can Italian whole peeled tomatoes, coarsely chopped
1 cup diced *serrano* ham or proscuitto
2 *chorizo* sausages, cut in rounds ⅓ in (1 cm) thick
12 eggs
24 pencil-thin asparagus spears, blanched
1 red bell pepper (capsicum), roasted, peeled, seeded and cut into strips (page 19)
1 tablespoon finely chopped parsley
freshly ground pepper

1. Fry the onion and garlic in olive oil for 3 minutes. Add the tomato and cook for 10 minutes.

2. Meanwhile, cook the ham and *chorizo* in a separate pan for 3 minutes.

3. Preheat oven to 400°F/200°C/Gas 6. Divide the tomato mixture among 6 individual ramekins. Break 2 eggs into each ramekin and then arrange the ham, *chorizo*, asparagus spears and pepper strips around them. Sprinkle with parsley and season with pepper. Bake until the whites of the eggs are cooked but the yolks are still runny, about 10 minutes. Serve right away.

SPICY HARD-BOILED EGGS
Huevos Duros Picantes
8 tapas servings

2 tablespoons olive oil
2 garlic cloves, finely chopped
2 teaspoons finely chopped ginger
1 onion, finely sliced
1 teaspoon cumin powder
1 teaspoon coriander (cilantro) powder
1 teaspoon turmeric
1 tablespoon chopped, seeded red chili
1½ cups/12 fl oz/375 ml unsweetened coconut milk
8 hard-boiled eggs, shelled
coriander (cilantro) sprigs

1. In a large pan, heat the oil and fry the garlic, ginger and onion until the onion is transparent. Add the powdered spices and the chili and cook for another 2 minutes, stirring constantly.

2. Remove from the heat and allow to cool. Blend in a food processor with the coconut milk. Return the mixture to the pan and bring to boil. Add the eggs, reduce the heat and simmer for 30 minutes, stirring occasionally. Serve garnished with coriander sprigs.

EGGS WITH TUNA MAYONNAISE
Huevos con Mayonesa de Atún
8 tapas servings

8 hard-boiled eggs, shelled and cut in half lengthwise
3 oz/100 g can tuna, drained
1 ½ cups/12 fl oz/375 ml mayonnaise (page 114)
1 tablespoon lemon juice
16 anchovy fillets
1 red bell pepper (capsicum) roasted and cut into strips (page 19)
watercress sprigs

Place two egg halves, yolk side down, on each serving plate. Force the tuna flesh through a fine sieve and whisk into the mayonnaise a little at a time until it is all combined. Add the lemon juice. Thickly coat the eggs with the tuna/mayonnaise mixture. Garnish with the anchovy fillets, the red bell pepper strips and watercress sprigs.

SALMON-STUFFED EGGS
Huevos Duros Rellenos
6 tapas servings

6 hard-boiled eggs
3 to 5 oz (100 to 150 g) can red salmon, drained
6 green olives, very finely chopped
2 tablespoons mayonnaise or garlic mayonnaise (page 114)
1 teaspoon paprika
1½ teaspoons chopped parsley
2 teaspoons lemon juice
salt and freshly ground pepper
1 slice smoked salmon, cut into thin strips
1 green bell pepper (capsicum), seeded and cut into thin strips

1. Halve the eggs neatly lengthwise and reserve 4 of the yolks for another use. Place the other 2 yolks in a bowl and add all remaining ingredients except the smoked salmon and bell pepper. Blend well.

2. Transfer to a piping (icing) bag and refill the egg whites with the mixture. Garnish with the smoked salmon and pepper.

SPANISH OMELETTE
Tortilla Española
12 to 16 tapas servings

The Spanish omelette is, without a doubt, the country's most commonly served dish. A true Spanish omelette contains only three ingredients–potatoes, onions and eggs – plus salt and the oil in which it is cooked. Despite its simplicity, it is uniquely delicious.

Spanish olive oil
5 potatoes, peeled and thinly sliced
2 large onions, thinly sliced
15 eggs
salt

1. In a heavy nonstick pan about 10 in (25 cm) wide and with sloping sides about 2 in (5 cm) deep, heat 2 tablespoons olive oil. (Adjust quantities of ingredients as necessary for another pan size.) The secret of this recipe is a very hot pan. When the oil begins to smoke, add the potato a few pieces at a time until the bottom is covered one layer deep. Top the potato with a layer of onion. Repeat until all the potato and onion are used. Cook, turning frequently, until the potato is tender, then remove the potato and onion from the pan. If anything has stuck to the pan, clean it thoroughly, add another tablespoon of oil and reheat until the oil is smoking.

2. Whip the eggs with a little salt. Mix into the cooked potatoes and onions. Pour the mixture into the pan and stir away from the bottom until half the egg is cooked, press the onion and potato down into the mixture. Shake the pan and run a spatula around the side and bottom to make sure the omelette is not sticking. When the omelette is cooked three-quarters of the way through and the bottom is browning (it musn't burn), place a large plate over the pan and invert the omelette onto it.

3. Quickly clean out the pan and add a little more olive oil. Slide the omelette back into the pan, uncooked side down, and cook until firm right through. Turn out onto a serving dish and let stand for 5 to 10 minutes before cutting into wedges. In Spain it is served lukewarm or at room temperature.

ZUCCHINI (COURGETTE) OMELETTE
Tortilla de Calabacines
12 tapas servings

10 to 13 oz/300 to 400 g zucchini (courgettes), sliced about ⅓ in
(1 cm) thick
12 eggs
salt and freshly ground pepper
2 tablespoons Spanish olive oil
½ cup/2 oz/60 g finely chopped onion
1 garlic clove, finely chopped or pressed

1. Steam the zucchini in a covered steamer set over boiling water for
about 3 minutes (or boil in ¾ in (2 cm) water for about the same time).
Drain. It must not be soggy!

2. Beat the eggs with salt and pepper. Heat 1 tablespoon of the oil in
a pan about 8 in (20 cm) wide and with sloping sides about 2 in (5 cm)
deep. Add the onion and garlic and sauté for 2 to 3 minutes; remove
and drain. Mix with the zucchini and egg.

3. Heat the remaining tablespoon of oil until smoking in the same pan.
Pour in the egg mixture and stir it away from the bottom 5 or 6 times.
Cook until the omelette is set two-thirds of the way through, place a large
plate over the pan and invert the omelette onto it.

4. Slide omelet back into the pan, uncooked side down, and cook until
set through. Divide into 12 equal portions and serve.

MUSHROOM OMELETTE
Tortilla de Champiñones
12 tapas servings

3 tablespoons Spanish olive oil
1 onion, finely chopped
1 lb/500 g mushrooms, cleaned and sliced
12 eggs

1. Heat 2 tablespoons olive oil in a pan about 8 in (20 cm) wide and with sloping sides about 2 in (5 cm) deep and sauté the onion and mushrooms 4 to 5 minutes. Meanwhile, beat the eggs with salt and pepper. Transfer the onions and mushrooms to a strainer lined with a paper towel and drain thoroughly, then add to the egg mixture.

2. Wipe the pan out, return to the heat with another tablespoon of oil and heat until smoking. Add the egg mixture and stir it away from the bottom 5 or 6 times. Cook until the omelette is set two-thirds of the way through, agitating the pan to make sure the egg doesn't stick.

3. Invert the omelette onto a large plate. Slide back into the pan, uncooked side down, and cook until set through. Divide into 12 equal portions and serve.

SPICY SHRIMP (PRAWN) OMELETTE
Tortilla de Gambas Picantes
8 tapas servings

3 tablespoons Spanish olive oil
2 large potatoes, peeled and thinly sliced
1 large onion, thinly sliced
15 eggs
1 teaspoon salt
4 red chilies, seeded and chopped, or 1 tablespoon *sambal oelek*
(page 115)
2 cups peeled and chopped jumbo shrimp (prawns)

1. Heat 2 tablespoons olive oil in a pan about 6 to 8 in (15 to 20 cm) wide and with sloping sides about 2 in (5 cm) deep. When the oil begins to smoke, spread half the potatoes evenly in the pan, top with the onion and then spread with the remaining potato. Turn the mixture frequently until the potatoes are cooked; take care not to burn them. Remove from heat.

2. Beat the eggs with the salt in a bowl large enough to hold all the ingredients. Stir in the chili, shrimp and potato mixture.

3. Wipe the pan clean, add the remaining tablespoon of oil and heat until smoking. Add the egg mixture and stir it away from the bottom of the pan 5 or 6 times. When the omelette is half-cooked, reduce heat, shake the pan and run a spatula around the side to prevent omelette sticking. When it is almost cooked, invert the omelette onto a large plate.

4. Return the pan to high heat, making sure there is nothing sticking to it and add more oil if necessary. Slide the omelette back into the pan, uncooked side down. Reduce heat and cook until the omelette is set through. Invert onto a plate and let stand for a few minutes before cutting into wedges. Serve warm or, as is more typical in Spain, at room temperature.

CLAMS IN PIQUANT TOMATO SAUCE
Almejas al Diablo
4 tapas servings

There is a great variety of shellfish in Spain; *almejas* are a type of clam, usually quite small. The following clam recipes are those used in Spain for this variety, so it is best to select the smallest type available at your market. Nevertheless, these dishes will reproduce perfectly well with larger clams. Just remember to reduce the number of clams you use according to their size.

1 onion, finely chopped
2 garlic cloves, finely chopped or pressed
olive oil
8 oz/250 g can Italian tomatoes, minced
1 or 2 red chilies, seeds removed
2 bay leaves
¼ cup/½ oz/15 g finely chopped parsley
1 cup/8 fl oz/250 ml dry white wine
salt and white pepper
36 small clams, cleaned

1. Fry the onion and garlic in a little olive oil until transparent. Add the tomatoes, chili, bay leaves, parsley, wine, salt and pepper and bring to boil over a high heat. Allow to reduce slightly.

2. Add the clams, cover the pan tightly and simmer until they have opened. Remove the clams as they open and discard any that remain closed.

3. Divide the clams among 4 serving bowls and cover with the sauce. Serve immediately.

Cleaning Clams
To eradicate the chance of ruining a perfectly good dish with sand released from clams during cooking, scrub the shells, place them in a container of lightly salted water and let stand overnight in a cool place.

CLAMS TARRAGONA STYLE
Almejas Romesco

4 tapas servings

2 red bell peppers (capsicums), roasted, seeded and cut into strips
(page 19)
½ cup/4 fl oz/125 ml red wine vinegar
olive oil
4 slices baguette (French bread), ⅜ in (1 cm) thick
4 or 5 garlic cloves, peeled
20 blanched almonds
½ cup/4 fl oz/125 ml dry white wine
2 red chilies, seeds removed
1 tablespoon finely chopped parsley
2 bay leaves
salt and freshly ground pepper
36 small clams, cleaned (page 51)
1 shot aguardiente (or grappa or cognac)
Fish Stock:
(Makes 1½ cups/12 fl oz/375 ml)
1 small cleaned whole fish (such as whiting or garfish), head on
½ cup/4 fl oz/125 ml white wine
2½ cups/20 fl oz/625 ml water
1 onion, quartered
6 black peppercorns, pinch of dried thyme

1. Marinate the pepper strips in the vinegar for several hours. Combine all the fish stock ingredients and simmer 1 hour. (Liquid will reduce to half.) Strain and reserve.

2. Drain the bell pepper and fry gently for a few minutes in 2 tablespoons olive oil. Fry the slices of bread and the garlic in the same oil. Combine bell pepper, garlic, almonds and fried bread in a blender or processor along with ½ cup/4 fl oz/125 ml fish stock and puree. Add 1 cup/8 fl oz/250 ml fish stock and the wine and blend until smooth.

3. Strain the mixture into a pan or casserole. Add the chilies, parsley, bay leaves, salt, pepper and clams and cook over a low heat, removing clams as they open. Cook the sauce another 5 minutes, then add the aguardiente and return the clams. Remove from heat immediately and serve, or leave covered for an hour or two and then gently reheat.

CLAMS IN WHITE WINE SAUCE
Almejas a la Marinera
4 tapas servings

This is, without doubt, the most frequently used method of cooking clams. There are very few tapas bars worth their salt around coastal Spain that do not have this dish on display.

olive oil
1 onion, finely chopped
6 garlic cloves, finely chopped or pressed
1 tablespoon flour
1 ½ cups/12 fl oz/375 ml medium-dry white wine
½ cup/1 oz/30 g minced parsley
1 chili, seeds removed
salt and freshly ground pepper
36 small clams, cleaned (page 51)

Heat a little oil in a pan, add the onion and garlic and cook until transparent. Stir in the flour and cook for 1 minute. Add all remaining ingredients except the clams and cook for 10 minutes. Add the clams and cook, removing them as they open; discard any that do not open. Sprinkle with a little more parsley and serve.

OYSTER PLATTER
Plato Variado de Ostras
6 *tapas servings*

36 oysters in the half shell
rock salt
3 teaspoons red caviar
3 teaspoons black caviar
1 Bloody Mary cocktail
1 lime
freshly ground pepper
½ cup/4 fl oz/125 ml prepared bechamel sauce
1 cup/2 oz/60 g finely chopped spinach leaves
½ cup/4 oz/120 g grated strong Cheddar cheese
3 teaspoons grated Parmesan cheese
1 tablespoon diced bacon
3 teaspoons Worcestershire sauce
parsley sprigs, lemon wedges

1. On a platter that is large enough to accommodate all 36 oysters, spread a layer of rock salt or suitable substitute which will allow the oysters to sit firmly without tilting and spilling their sauces.

2. Arrange 18 of the oysters on the platter. Place ½ teaspoon of the red caviar on 6 oysters, covering half of each oyster, and ½ teaspoon black caviar on the other half. Top up the shells of the next 6 oysters with the Bloody Mary. Squeeze the lime juice over the last 6 oysters and top with a little pepper.

3. Place the remaining 18 oysters on a broiling (grilling) tray. Mix half the bechamel sauce with half the Cheddar cheese in a pot and heat gently until the cheese has melted and combined with the sauce. Spoon mixture over 6 oysters and top with Parmesan cheese.

4. Blanch the spinach in boiling water for 2 minutes. Drain and squeeze dry. Combine spinach with the remaining bechamel and Cheddar in a pot and heat gently until the cheese has melted. Spoon mixture over 6 oysters. Top the remaining 6 oysters with diced bacon and a few drops of Worcestershire sauce.

5. Place the tray under the broiler (griller) and cook until the sauces begin to brown and bubble. Arrange on the platter with the other 18 oysters, garnish with parsley sprigs and lemon wedges and serve.

MUSSELS WITH GARLIC MAYONNAISE
Mejillones al alïoli
10 tapas servings

40 mussels, scrubbed and debearded
2 lemon slices
1 ½ cups/ 12 fl oz/375 ml garlic mayonnaise (page 114)
1 bell pepper (capsicum), roasted, peeled, seeded and finely sliced
(page 19)
parsley sprigs

1. Steam the mussels in about 2 in (5 cm) water with the lemon slices, removing them as they open. Refresh the mussels under cold water. Discard the half shells to which the mussels are not attached.

2. Arrange the mussels on a platter in the remaining half shells, top with garlic mayonnaise and garnish with the pepper and parsley.

MUSSELS MARINATED IN VINAIGRETTE SAUCE
Mejillones en Escabeche
8 tapas servings

40 mussels, scrubbed and debearded
Escabeche:
1½ cups/12 fl oz/375 ml olive oil
¾ cup/6 fl oz/175 ml red wine vinegar
½ cup/2 oz/60 g minced onion
1 tablespoon chopped parsley
2 teaspoons hot paprika or chili powder
juice of 1 lemon
salt and freshly ground pepper

1. Steam the mussels in about 2 in (5 cm) water, removing them as they open. Refresh under cold water and discard the half shells to which the mussels are not attached.

2. Mix the *escabeche* ingredients together and add the mussels. Refrigerate for at least 12 hours, preferably 24. Serve the mussels cold in their marinade.

MUSSELS IN TOMATO SAUCE
Mejillones Madrileños
8 tapas servings

40 mussels, scrubbed and debearded
3 tablespoons olive oil
1 onion, finely chopped
4 garlic cloves, finely chopped or pressed
1 lb/465 g can Italian whole peeled tomatoes
½ cup/1 oz/30 g chopped parsley
2 bay leaves
salt and freshly ground pepper
a sprinkling of grated Parmesan cheese

1. Steam the mussels in about 2 in (5 cm) water, removing them as they open. Refresh under cold water and set aside. Discard the half shells to which the mussels are not attached.

2. Heat the olive oil in a large pan and sauté the onion and garlic until transparent. Add remaining ingredients except the cheese and boil until reduced to a smooth sauce.

3. Arrange the mussels on a baking sheet. Cover each mussel with some of the tomato sauce. Top with a sprinkling of Parmesan cheese and brown under the broiler (griller). Serve at once.

MUSSELS IN RUM SAUCE
Mejillones con Salsa de Ron
6 tapas servings

The sauce for this dish originates with a Caribbean method of cooking crabs. It is very popular when adapted this way for cooking mussels.

48 mussels, scrubbed and bearded
1 qt/1 l fresh cream
2 teaspoons finely chopped thyme
2 teaspoons finely chopped basil
2 teaspoons finely chopped oregano
½ cup/4 fl oz/125 ml dark rum
3 teaspoons freshly ground pepper

1. Put all the ingredients except the rum and the pepper into a pot with a tight-fitting lid, and cook over high heat until the mussels have opened, about 3 to 5 minutes.

2. Remove the lid and add the rum and the pepper. Ignite the rum and cook until the flame dies. Serve immediately in individual bowls.

STEAMED MUSSELS IN GAZPACHO
Mejillones en Gazpacho Andaluz
8 tapas servings

Garnish these with chopped bell pepper (capsicum) and garlic-fried croutons.

1 lb/465 can Italian whole peeled tomatoes
1 large green bell pepper (capsicum), seeded and coarsely chopped
1 medium onion, coarsely chopped
2 small cucumbers, peeled, seeded and chopped
2 tablespoons tarragon vinegar
3 garlic cloves, peeled
1 cup/6 oz/180 g crushed ice
salt and freshly ground pepper
2¼ lb/1 kg mussels, scrubbed and debearded

1. Combine all ingredients except the mussels in a blender and puree. Force the resulting mixture through a sieve with the aid of a wooden spoon. Check the seasoning, then cover tightly with plastic wrap and refrigerate overnight.

2. Place the mussels in a pot with about ¾ in (2 cm) of water. Cover and set over high heat. Checking every minute or so, remove opened mussels and refresh under cold water. Divide the mussels among 8 serving bowls and pour the chilled gazpacho over them.

SCALLOPS WITH BACON AND GARLIC
Vieiras San Ricardo

8 tapas servings

1 cup diced *tocino*, pancetta or bacon (speck)
1 cup/8 oz/250 g garlic butter
24 scallops on the half shell, coral removed
lemon wedges

Distribute the *tocino* and garlic butter evenly among the scallops. Arrange on a broiler (grill) tray and place under a hot broiler (grill) for about 4 minutes or until half-cooked; if cooked through, the scallops will become dry and rubber. Serve with lemon wedges.

Garlic Butter: To make garlic butter finely chop 6 garlic cloves, add to 1 cup/8 oz/250 g softened butter with 1 tablespoon finely chopped parsley.

SCALLOPS IN THE SHELL WITH GARLIC, GINGER AND LIME

Vieiras con Ajo, Jengibre y Lima

8 tapas servings

juice of 4 limes
3 tablespoons white wine
2 red chilies, seeded and finely chopped
24 scallops on the half shell
6 tablespoons olive oil
julienned fresh ginger (about 4 or 5 matchsticks per scallop)
8 garlic cloves, thinly sliced crosswise

1. Mix the lime juice, wine and chili and divide evenly among the scallops on their shells. Marinate the scallops for at least 1 hour; the lime juice will ''bleach'' the scallops. (If you prefer, you can remove the scallops from their shells, then return them with about 1 teaspoon marinade after they are marinated. In either case, there should be only about a teaspoon of marinade left in the shell when you proceed to the next stage.)

2. Heat the olive oil in a small pan and fry the ginger and garlic until golden and crunchy. Arrange the scallops on a broiler (grill) tray and place under a preheated broiler (grill) only until heated through. Top each scallop with a sprinkling of garlic and ginger. Serve immediately.

SCALLOPS WITH PIMIENTO
Vieiras con Pimiento
8 tapas servings

2 red bell peppers (capsicums), roasted, seeded and cut into strips (page 19)
2 tablespoons extra virgin olive oil
2 tablespoons red wine vinegar
24 scallops on the half shell
24 teaspoons dry white wine
coarsely ground black pepper
2 tablespoons freshly grated Parmesan cheese
lemon or lime wedges

1. Marinate the bell pepper strips in the olive oil and vinegar for at least 30 minutes. Crisscross two or more strips over each scallop and drizzle with a teaspoon of wine. Grind a little black pepper over each scallop and sprinkle with a little Parmesan cheese.

2. Broil the scallops under a preheated broiler (grill) for 4 to 5 minutes, taking care not to overcook them. Serve with lemon or lime wedges.

MUSSELS STEAMED IN SPICY TOMATO SAUCE
Mejillones Mediterrasia
8 tapas servings

Serve these with warm, crusty bread to soak up the sauce.

2 onions, finely chopped
6 garlic cloves, finely chopped
1 tablespoon finely chopped fresh ginger
1 bunch coriander (cilantro), roots and leaves finely chopped
separately
2 tablespoons olive oil
1 lb/465 g can Italian whole peeled tomatoes, pureed
1 tablespoon *sambal oelek* (page 115)
1 ¼ cups/10 fl oz/300 ml dry white wine
salt
2 ¼ lb/1 kg mussels, scrubbed and debearded
coriander (cilantro) sprigs
finely sliced green and yellow bell pepper (capsicum)

1. In a pot large enough to accommodate all the ingredients, sauté the onion, garlic, ginger and chopped coriander root in the olive oil for 3 to 4 minutes. Add the tomatoes, *sambal*, wine and salt to taste and simmer for about 10 minutes. Add the chopped coriander leaves and the mussels. Increase the heat and cover tightly.

2. Have 8 small serving bowls ready. As the mussels open, remove them from the pot and divide them among the dishes, checking the pot every 2 minutes (if the opened mussels are allowed to remain in the liquid, the flesh will shrink and toughen). It will take from 6 to 10 minutes for all to open; discard any that do not open after this time.

3. Pour the sauce over the mussels. Garnish with coriander sprigs and green and yellow pepper slices, and serve.

CRAB SALAD IN THE SHELL
Ensalada de Cangrejo
8 tapas servings

For this recipe I always try to buy uncooked crabs and cook them myself. Simply boil or steam them in a little water to which a tablespoon of vinegar is added. After 5 minutes remove one of the crab's shell and check whether the meat is white and cooked through. Take care not to overcook them as the flesh will become mushy. Refresh them in cold water instantly. If only cooked crabs are available, check them for freshness and make sure they have hard shells.

8 cooked medium-size blue swimmer crabs (about ¼ lb/250 g), or
equal weight cooked crabmeat
2 medium onions, finely diced
2 celery stalks, finely diced
4 green chilies, seeded and finely diced
1 large tomato, seeded and finely diced
1 avocado, peeled and diced
1 cup/8 fl oz/250 ml garlic mayonnaise (page 114)
salt
16 pimento-stuffed green olives
½ red bell pepper (capsicum), seeded and finely diced
lettuce leaves

1. Remove the shells from the crabs, taking care not to break them. Clean them out thoroughly. Break the claws and the legs from the crab bodies and set aside. Discard any roe and the feathery lungs from the crab bodies, then carefully extract the meat. Place this in a bowl and add all the remaining ingredients except the olives, bell pepper and lettuce.

2. Spoon the mixture into the cleaned crab shells and place each one on a bed of lettuce. Rearrange the claws and legs around the shell. (I always crack the claws and reassemble them for ease of handling.) As the finishing touch, set the stuffed olives into the salad mixture to resemble eyes. Garnish with red pepper.

SPICY CRAB AND SHRIMP (PRAWNS)
Cangrejo y Gambas a la India
8 tapas servings

If any of this is left over, keep it as an ideal filling for empanadas (page 111).

8 cooked medium-size blue swimmer crabs (about ½ lb/250 g), or equal weight cooked crabmeat (see page 64 for cooking instructions)
1 onion, finely chopped
6 garlic cloves, finely chopped
1 ½ teaspoons finely chopped fresh ginger
1 ½ teaspoons finely chopped coriander (cilantro) roots
1 tablespoon butter
1 tablespoon flour
¾ cup/6 fl oz/175 ml unsweetened coconut milk
1 tablespoon *sambal oelek* (page 115)
16 large shrimp (prawns), cooked, peeled and chopped
¼ cup/1 oz/60 g hot steamed white rice
1 tablespoon chopped coriander (cilantro) leaves

1. Remove the crab shells and clean thoroughly; set the crab flesh aside. Remove the flesh from the claws as well.

2. Fry the onion, garlic, ginger and coriander root in the butter for 3 to 4 minutes. Stir in the flour and cook for a further minute. Gradually stir in the coconut milk and the *sambal oelek* and cook for 5 minutes. Remove from heat and add the shrimp and crabmeat.

3. Put half a tablespoon of cooked rice in each shell. Spoon in the seafood mixture. Garnish with the chopped coriander leaves.

GRILLED SHRIMP (PRAWNS)
Gambas a la Plancha
8 tapas servings

A la plancha simply means that the item is grilled on a griddle or hot plate, a very common method of cooking seafood and steaks in Spain. The best way to duplicate the effect is to use a large, very heavy pan that has been lightly oiled, with further small amounts of oil added during cooking. (The shrimp can only be cooked a few at a time, as each one must rest on the bottom of the pan.) Alternatively, the shrimp can be cooked on a barbecue hot plate (my preferred method) or on the barbecue itself, basted with olive oil and garlic. *A la plancha* is probably the most common method of cooking shrimp in Spain, where they are usually eaten from the shell.

8 garlic cloves, coarsely chopped
½ cup/4 fl oz/125 ml olive oil
2 ¼ lb/1 kg shrimp (prawns), washed but unpeeled
chopped parsley
garlic mayonnaise (page 114)

1. Marinate the garlic in the olive oil for at least 30 minutes.

2. Oil a large pan or hot plate and heat over medium high heat. Add as many shrimp as will fit in one layer. Pour about a teaspoon of olive oil over each of the shrimp and add some of the garlic. Cook for 2 minutes, then turn the shrimp over. Drizzle with a little more olive oil and cook for 2 more minutes, then remove from heat. (Do not overcook or shrimp will become mushy.)

3. If you are using a pan, wipe it out with a paper towel and repeat the process until all the shrimp are cooked. Keep the cooked shrimp warm under a broiler (grill) turned down very low (or in a low oven) while you cook the remainder. Sprinkle with chopped parsley and serve wth garlic mayonnaise.

GARLIC SHRIMP (PRAWNS)
Gambas al Ajillo
8 tapas servings

Serve with plenty of crusty bread.

2 ¼ lb/1 kg shrimp (prawns), peeled and deveined
8 garlic cloves, finely chopped
4 red chilies, seeded and chopped
olive oil
coarse salt

1. Divide the garlic and chilies among 8 individual, flameproof earthenware or metal ramekins. To each ramekin add enough olive oil to just cover the shrimp that will be added. Heat over a high flame until the garlic turns golden brown.

2. Add the shrimp and remove from heat after 1 minute. Sprinkle with coarse salt and serve immediately.

CHILI SHRIMP (PRAWNS) WITH CREAM SAUCE

Gambas Picantes con Nata

8 tapas servings

I always prepare this dish in a large covered wok. The flavors of the chili, garlic and ginger permeate the shrimp, and the juice exuded by the shrimp greatly enhances the sauce. This is an all-time favorite in my household.

2 tablespoons olive oil
24 unpeeled large shrimp (prawns)
1 tablespoon finely chopped ginger
1 tablespoon finely chopped garlic
1 tablespoon *sambal oelek* (page 115)
1¼ cups/10 fl oz/310 ml heavy (thick) cream

1. Heat a wok over a high flame, adding 1 tablespoon olive oil. When oil is smoking, add half the shrimp, half the ginger and half the garlic all at once. Stir for 1 minute, then cover and cook for 3 to 4 minutes or until the shrimp are just cooked through; don't overcook. Remove and repeat with the remaining shrimp, ginger and garlic; remove from the wok.

2. Add the *sambal* and cream to the wok and bring to boil; let boil for 4 to 5 minutes to reduce. Tip the sauce into a bowl and serve as a dipping mixture for the shrimp (have diners peel their own). Don't forget the fingerbowls.

SHRIMP (PRAWNS) IN SHERRY SAUCE
Gambas al Jerez
8 tapas servings

2 tablespoons butter
1 lb/500 g shrimp (prawns), peeled
1 tablespoon flour
2 tablespoons Dijon mustard
¼ cup/2 fl oz/60 ml dry sherry
¾ cup/6 fl oz/175 ml fresh cream
¾ cup/6 fl oz/175 ml fish stock

In a pan, brown the shrimp quickly in the butter. Tip off any excess liquid but leave a little to make the sauce. Add the flour and mix thoroughly, then add the mustard and the sherry and cook for 1 minute. Pour in the cream and the fish stock. Stir until the shrimp are cooked and the sauce has a smooth consistency, about 1 or 2 minutes. Serve immediately.

CHILI SHRIMP (PRAWNS) IN A LETTUCE BOAT
Gambas Picantes en Barco

8 tapas servings

2 tablespoons olive oil
1 onion, finely chopped
1 ½ teaspoons finely chopped garlic
1 tablespoon *sambal oelek* (page 115), or 4 red chilies, seeded and finely chopped
1 lb/500 g peeled large shrimp (prawns), halved lengthwise
2 tablespoons chopped lean bacon
2 tablespoons cognac
2 green (spring) onions, green tops included, finely chopped
1 ½ teaspoons cornstarch (cornflour)
½ cup/4 fl oz/125 ml water
1 tablespoon soy sauce
oil for frying
2 oz/50 g Chinese vermicelli
8 firm inner lettuce leaves, trimmed to form a cup

1. Heat the olive oil in a large pan or wok until it is beginning to smoke. Add the onion, garlic and *sambal* and cook for 1 minute. Add the shrimp, bacon and cognac and ignite, shaking the pan gently until the flames subside. Add the green onion and then the cornstarch and mix well. Pour in the water and soy sauce and cook for 3 minutes or until smooth and slightly thickened. Remove from heat.

2. In another pan heat 1 cup/8 fl oz/250 ml oil until it is quite hot. Roughly pull apart the strands of vermicelli and fry in several batches; the noodles will puff up immediately. Drain the noddles on paper towels.

3. Place a spoonful of the shrimp mixture into each lettuce cup, top with the vermicelli and serve immediately.

SHRIMP (PRAWN) COCKTAIL

Cóctel de Gambas

6 tapas servings

6 cups/1 ½ qt/1.5 l water
parsley sprigs
6 peppercorns
pinch of salt
1 lb/500 g unshelled shrimp (prawns)
1 cup garlic mayonnaise (page 114)
1 ½ tablespoons ketchup (tomato sauce)
6 green olives, very finely chopped
1 hard-boiled egg, finely chopped
2 teaspoons Spanish brandy or cognac
1 ½ teaspoons chopped parsley
freshly ground pepper
chopped onion (optional), lettuce, paprika, lemon twists

1. Combine the water, 2 parsley sprigs, peppercorns and salt and bring to boil. Boil for 5 minutes, then add the shrimp and cook for 3 to 4 minutes. Drain and refresh under cold water. Peel and cut in half lengthwise.

2. Combine the mayonnaise, ketchup, olives, egg, brandy, chopped parsley and pepper. Add the cooled shrimp. Serve in cocktail glasses over a bed of combined chopped onion and lettuce, or serve on individual lettuce leaves. Garnish with a sprinkling of paprika, lemon twists and parsley sprigs.

LOBSTER AND PEPPER SALAD
Ensalada de Langosta y trés Pimientos
6 to 8 tapas servings

2 red bell peppers (capsicums)
1 yellow bell pepper (capsicum)
1 green bell pepper (capsicum)
flesh from 1 ½ lb/750 g lobster, diced
2 tablespoons chopped parsley
3 tablespoons olive oil
2 tablespoons lemon juice
salt and freshly ground black pepper
watercress sprigs
lemon wedges

1. Roast and cut the peppers into strips as described on page 19. Mix the lobster flesh together with the peppers and the parsley.

2. Whisk the olive oil, lemon juice, salt and pepper together. Dress the salad, then refrigerate it for 30 minutes. Serve garnished with watercress and lemon wedges. Lobster legs in the shell can be used as an additional garnish.

STUFFED LOBSTER TAILS
Langosta Rellena
8 tapas servings

The slipper lobster tails used in this recipe are available from fish markets in frozen form. They are smaller than the average lobster or crayfish tail and range in size from 3 oz (100 g). Small ones are required for this recipe.

8 slipper lobster tails
2 onions, finely chopped
4 garlic cloves, finely chopped
1 tablespoon finely chopped fresh ginger
2 tablespoons chopped coriander (cilantro), including roots
4 green (spring) onions, including green tops, finely chopped
¼ cup/2 fl oz/60 ml olive oil
½ cup/4 fl oz/125 ml cognac
1 tablespoon hot paprika
2 tablespoons *sambal oelek* (page 115)
4 red bell peppers (capsicums), roasted, peeled, seeded and pureed (page 19)
1 cup/8 oz/250 g whole peeled tomatoes, pureed
2 tablespoons red wine vinegar
2 tablespoons butter

1. Pull the flesh from each lobster tail, leaving the shell intact. Blanch the shells in boiling water for 2 to 3 minutes and clean them. Remove the tough outer skin from the lobster flesh and cut the flesh into ½ to ¾ in (1 to 2 cm) cross-sections.

2. Sauté the onion, garlic, ginger, coriander root and the white part of the green onions in olive oil for 4 minutes. Add the cognac and boil 1 minute. Add the paprika, *sambal*, pepper puree, tomato puree and vinegar and simmer 15 to 20 minutes.

3. In another pan melt the butter and gently sauté the lobster pieces with the green onion tops and the coriander leaves. When the lobster pieces have changed color and are half cooked, drain off the butter and add the lobster to the simmering sauce. The minute the lobster pieces are opaque all the way through (do not overcook), remove them from the sauce and arrange them in the shells. Spoon the sauce over and serve.

MIXED SEAFOOD VINAIGRETTE
Salpicón
20 tapas servings

For a dramatic presentation, top this with a whole cooked lobster, or with whole cooked shrimp (prawns) or crabs in their shells.

1 cup/8 fl oz/250 ml olive oil
juice of 1 lemon
⅓ cup/2 ½ fl oz/80 ml white wine vinegar
½ cup/2 oz/60 g finely chopped onion
2 bell peppers (capsicums), roasted, peeled, seeded and cut into
thin strips (page 19)
1 lb/500 g cooked lobster
1 lb/500 g cooked shrimp (prawns)
7 oz/200 g cooked crabmeat
7 oz/200 g cooked mussels
7 oz/200 g cleaned squid, cut into rings, poached for 1 minute in
white wine and drained
7 oz/200 g cooked firm, white-fleshed fish

Combine the olive oil, lemon juice, vinegar, onion and peppers in a large bowl and mix well. Fold in the mixed seafood. Cover and refrigerate several hours or overnight, turning occasionally. Serve chilled.

SEAFOOD MEDLEY
Zarzuela Tapa
8 tapas servings

4 medium blue swimmer crabs, raw or cooked (about ¼ lb/125 g),
or equal quantity crabmeat
2 tablespoons olive oil
1 onion, finely diced
4 garlic cloves, finely chopped
8 raw jumbo shrimp (prawns), unpeeled
8 oz/250 g tuna or other firm-fleshed fish, such as cod, cut into
¾ in/2 cm cubes
1 cup/8 fl oz/250 ml fish stock
1 lb/465 g can Italian whole peeled tomatoes
3 red chilies, seeded and chopped, or 1 tablespoon *sambal oelek*
(page 115)
¼ cup/2 fl oz/60 ml cognac
½ cup/4 fl oz/125 ml dry white wine
1 tablespoon chopped parsley
32 fresh mussels, scrubbed and debearded
salt

1. Clean the crabs and cut them down the center so that each half has
a claw attached. Set aside.

2. Heat the olive oil in a large pan. Sauté the onion and garlic for 2
minutes, then add the shrimp, crabs (if raw) and fish cubes. Add about
half the fish stock and simmer the mixture, removing the seafood as it
is almost cooked. When all seafood has been removed, add the remaining
fish stock to the pan with the tomatoes, chilies, cognac, wine and parsley
and simmer for 10 minutes. Add the mussels and cook, removing them
as they open.

3. Divide the mussels among 8 serving bowls. Return the crab (raw or
cooked), shrimp and fish to the simmering sauce and cook 2 minutes.
Divide the seafood and sauce among the bowls and serve at once.

GRILLED SQUID
Calamares a la Plancha
8 to 10 tapas servings

This is one of the simplest, commonest and most effective methods of preparing squid. On Spanish menus one often encounters the term *a la plancha*, which simply means that the food was grilled on a *plancha* or griddle. Since this is not standard equipment in most kitchens, the best way to achieve the same results is to use a large, heavy pan or skillet that has been coated with oil. You may also have a barbecue equipped with a hot plate. Use moderate to high heat.

15 to 20 small squid
2 to 3 tablespoons olive oil
3 garlic cloves, finely chopped or pressed
1 tablespoon chopped parsley

1. Clean the squid as described in the recipe for *Calamares en su Tinta* (page 79). Replace the tentacles in the cleaned bodies. Heat a pan or skillet and add half the olive oil and half the garlic. Put in the squid and cook on one side for 3 to 4 minutes. Remove the squid, clean out the pan with a paper towel and then return the squid to the pan, uncooked side down. Add the remainder of the olive oil and garlic and cook for 3 minutes. Serve garnished with parsley.

2. If cooking on a barbecue hot plate, employ the same "double-cooking" method described for *Pulpo a la Plancha* on page 83.

DEEP-FRIED SQUID
Calamares a la Romana
8 tapas servings

This particular Spanish dish has become an international favorite and needs little introduction. The recipe below is just one of many variations, but it is the one I found most popular with my clientele in Spain.

If you are buying whole fresh squid pull out the tentacles; remove the wings, ink sacs, spine and guts, and rinse out the insides thoroughly. Keep the tentacles and wings for *Calamares Pica-Pica* (page 78) and the ink sacs for *Calamares en su Tinta* (page 79).

2¼ lb/1 kg fresh squid, cleaned
flour for dredging
4 eggs mixed with 2 cups/16 fl oz/500 ml water
breadcrumbs
oil for frying

1. Slice the squid into rings about ¼ in (½ cm) thick. Dredge the rings in flour, dip into the egg mixture and coat with the breadcrumbs.

2. The major secret of successful *Calamares a la Romana* is the heat of the oil and the speed at which they are cooked. They should be deep-fried at 350 to 400°F (180 to 200°C) for no more than 1 minute; this ensures that they will be tender. If they are cooked for any longer they tend to become rubbery. Note also that the smaller the squid, the more tender they are likely to be.

SQUID IN SPICY RED SAUCE
Calamares Pica-Pica
6 tapas servings

The tentacles and wings discarded from the recipe for *Calamares a la Romana* (page 77) are the basic ingredient for *Calamares Pica-Pica* (which in idiomatic Spanish means spicy "hot-hot"). You may add more finely chopped squid to make up the quantity, if required.

2 tablespoons olive oil
1 onion, finely chopped
2 garlic cloves, finely chopped or pressed
8 oz/250 g finely diced squid tentacles and wings
1 tablespoon flour
½ cup/4 fl oz/125 ml dry red wine
3 or 4 chopped chilies, seeds removed, or 4 teaspoons chili powder, or 1 tablespoon *sambal oelek* (page 115)
salt and freshly ground pepper
1 teaspoon paprika
juice of 1 lemon

1. Heat the olive oil in a pan and sauté the onion and garlic until transparent. Add the squid and fry for 1 minute, stirring constantly. Remove from heat and stir in the flour.

2. Return to the heat and cook for 2 minutes, then add the wine, chilies, salt, pepper and paprika. Simmer for about 45 minutes or until the squid is tender. Add the lemon juice before serving.

BABY SQUID IN ITS OWN INK
Calamares en su Tinta
6 tapas servings

This dish is best prepared with baby squid up to 4 in (10 cm) long, but generally the quantity of small squid used will not produce enough ink for the preparation of the dish. The solution is to save the ink sacs—found just behind the tentacles—from squid that are being used for *Calamares a la Romana, Pica-Pica* or *Calamares Rellenos* and freeze them to use in this dish. Alternatively, you can buy some larger squid, extract the ink sacs and freeze the rest for later use.

1 lb/500 g baby squid, plus ink sacs from 2 large squid
½ cup/4 fl oz/125 ml dry red wine
olive oil
1 onion, finely chopped
1 garlic clove, finely chopped or pressed
1 tablespoon flour
1 tomato, peeled and chopped
1 cup/8 fl oz/250 ml fish stock or clam juice
salt and freshly ground pepper

1. Clean the squid by removing the tentacles and taking out the ink sacs (keep these). Discard the hard "beak" at the base of the tentacles. Clean out the inside of the squid and remove any purple skin from the outside. When the body is cleaned, stuff the tentacles back into it.

2. Put the ink sacs, plus those you have saved from other squid, in a strainer and scrape them over a bowl with a wooden spoon. Pour some of the wine through the strainer and scrape again. Repeat this process several times until you have slightly less than ¾ cup/6 fl oz/175 ml of liquid.

3. Heat a little olive oil in a pan and fry the onion and garlic until transparent. Stir in the flour and cook for 1 minute. Add the tomato, stock, ink mixture, salt, pepper and squid and simmer, covered, for 30 to 40 minutes or until the squid is tender. Serve hot in the sauce.

STUFFED BABY SQUID
Calamares Rellenos
8 to 10 tapas servings

15 to 20 small squid
olive oil
1 onion, finely chopped
3 garlic cloves, finely chopped or pressed
7 oz/200 g chopped *serrano* ham or prosciutto
1 tablespoon chopped parsley
2 tablespoons dry white wine
½ cup/2 oz/60 g breadcrumbs
salt and freshly ground pepper
flour
Simple Tomato Sauce (see page 97)

1. Clean the squid well (see previous recipe). Heat a little olive oil in a pan and fry the onion and garlic until transparent. Add the ham and cook for 1 minute. Remove from heat and add the parsley, wine, breadcrumbs, salt and pepper. Stuff the squid bodies ⅔ full with this mixture.

2. Replace the tentacles in the body opening, dust with flour and quickly brown in hot olive oil.

3. Preheat oven to 350°F/180°C/Gas 4. Transfer squid to a baking dish and cover with tomato sauce. Cover the dish and bake 1 hour or until the squid are completely tender. Serve hot.

STUFFED BABY SQUID II
Calamares Rellenos II

8 to 10 tapas servings

15 to 20 small squid
1 onion, finely chopped
4 garlic cloves, finely chopped
1 tablespoon olive oil
1 tablespoon flour
1 tablespoon roasted red pepper (capsicum)
7 oz/200 g chopped cooked mussel meat
3 oz/100 g blanched shrimp (prawns)
5 oz/155 g can clams, drained
10 pimento-stuffed green olives, finely chopped
1 tablespoon chopped parsley
salt and freshly ground pepper
2 eggs, lightly beaten
½ cup/2 oz/60 g fresh breadcrumbs
2 red bell peppers (capsicums), roasted, seeded and cut into strips
(page 19)
seasoned flour for dredging
1 cup/8 fl oz/250 ml olive oil
1 tablespoon chopped fresh basil
1 tablespoon chopped garlic

1. Clean the squid well (see recipe for *Calamares en su Tinta*, page 79). Sauté the onion and garlic in 1 tablespoon olive oil for 2 to 3 minutes. Stir in the flour and cook for 1 minute. Add the pepper puree, mussel meat, shrimp, clams, olives, parsley, salt and pepper and cook for 1 minute, stirring. Remove from heat and allow the mixture to cool.

2. Add the eggs, breadcrumbs and pepper strips. Stuff the squid bodies ⅔ full with the mixture. Replace the tentacles in the body opening, dredge the squid in seasoned flour and fry for 2 minutes in olive oil to which the basil and garlic have been added.

3. Transfer the squid to a baking dish. Spoon the olive oil, garlic and basil over the squid and bake at 350°F/180°C/Gas 4 for 30 to 45 minutes or until the squid are tender. Allow to cool. Slice crosswise and arrange on a platter. Serve at room temperature.

SQUID AND OCTOPUS SALAD
Ensalada de Calamares y Pulpo
8 to 10 tapas servings

3 ¼ lb/1.5 kg tenderized baby octopus (page 114)
3 ¼ lb/1.5 kg fresh squid (cheaper varieties of squid will do for this recipe)
1 cup/8 fl oz/250 ml white wine vinegar
1 onion studded with 12 cloves
6 bay leaves
12 white peppercorns
1 teaspoon salt
1 tablespoon finely chopped fresh dill
1 cup/8 fl oz/250 ml olive oil
½ cup/4 fl oz/125 ml freshly squeezed lemon juice
lettuce leaves
lemon wedges
freshly ground pepper

1. Clean the octopus, removing and discarding the heads. Clean the squid thoroughly, discarding the heads but retaining the tentacles. Bring 3 to 4 quarts/liters of water to boil. Add the vinegar, clove-studded onion, bay leaves and peppercorns and boil for about 10 minutes. Add the squid and octopus and boil for 20 to 30 minutes or until tender. Refresh in cold water and remove any skin from the seafood. Discard the other contents of the pot. Cut the octopus and squid tentacles into chunks and slice the squid bodies into very fine rings.

2. Mix the seafood with the dill, olive oil and lemon juice and marinate overnight in the refrigerator. Serve on a lettuce leaf with lemon wedges and pepper.

Variation: I sometimes vary this recipe as follows: substitute lime juice for the lemon juice and fresh coriander (cilantro) for dill; add 1 tablespoon *sambal oelek* (page 115) to the marinade.

BARBECUED BABY OCTOPUS
Pulpo a la Plancha
8 tapas servings

Anyone who has spent any time in the Mediterranean or Aegean will recall the sight of locals bashing freshly caught octopus against the rocks to tenderize it. Elsewhere it is often possible to buy baby octopus that has already been tenderized. There is an easy way to tell whether octopus has been tenderized. If it has, the tentacles will be balled up like a fist; if it hasn't, they will hang limply when you pick it up.

This method of double-cooking the octopus ensures that it is evenly grilled, crisp and flavored with the oil and garlic. If you only cook it once it stews in its own juices, and if it is cooked over the open flame of the barbecue it tends to dry out.

1 cup/8 fl oz/250 ml olive oil
4 garlic cloves, finely chopped
4½ lb/2 kg tenderized baby octopus (page 114)
¼ cup/2 fl oz/60 ml lemon juice
Sweet Chili Sauce (page 42)

1. Combine the olive oil and garlic and set aside for several hours.

2. Remove and discard the octopus heads (some people clean them out and use them but I don't think they're worth the bother). Remove the little hard ball, or "beak", in the center of each octopus.

3. Heat a griddle over hot coals until very hot. Evenly cover it with half the oil-and-garlic mixture. Place all the octopus on the hot plate and sprinkle with the lemon juice (a lot of liquid will exude from the octopus and the hot plate will cool down considerably). Cook for about 2 minutes on each side or until the octopus is barely cooked through.

4. Remove the octopus and scrape down the plate; allow it to heat up again. When very hot, cover it with the other half of the oil-and-garlic mixture. When the oil begins to smoke, grill the octopus underside down until the ends of the tentacles are crunchy. Serve immediately with Sweet Chili Sauce.

OCTOPUS GALICIAN STYLE
Pulpo a la Gallega
10 tapas servings

4½ lb/2 kg tenderized baby octopus (page 114)
2 qt/2 l water
1 onion, peeled
1 bay leaf
6 black peppercorns
1 cup/8 fl oz/250 ml olive oil
1 tablespoon hot paprika, or a mixture of paprika and chili powder,
or *sambal oelek* (page 115)
coarse sea salt and freshly ground pepper

1. Clean the octopus thoroughly; discard the heads.

2. Bring the water to boil. Add the octopus, onion, bay leaf and peppercorns and simmer until the octopus is tender, about 20 to 30 minutes. Drain and cool.

3. Mix the olive oil and seasonings in a bowl and add the octopus. Refrigerate overnight.

4. Remove octopus from the marinade and place on a broiler (grilling) pan. Broil (grill) for 2 to 3 minutes on each side. Serve with a sprinkling of marinade and additional paprika and coarse salt.

OCTOPUS IN VINAIGRETTE
Pulpo en Escabeche
10 tapas servings

4½ lb/2 kg tenderized baby octopus (page 114)
2 qt/2 l water
1 onion, peeled
1 bay leaf
6 black peppercorns
1 cup/8 fl oz/250 ml olive oil
¼ cup/2 fl oz/60 ml red wine vinegar
½ cup/2 oz/60 g finely chopped onion
2 garlic cloves, finely chopped or pressed
1 bay leaf
2 teaspoons hot paprika
salt and freshly ground pepper

1. Clean the octopus thoroughly; discard the heads.

2. Bring the water to boil. Add the octopus, onion, bay leaf and peppercorns, and simmer until the octopus is tender, about 20 to 30 minutes. Drain and cool under cold running water. Cut into pieces.

3. Combine the olive oil, vinegar, onion, garlic, bay leaf, paprika and seasonings in a large bowl. Add the octopus and refrigerate at least 12 hours, preferably longer. Serve chilled.

FISH PUFFS
Buñuelos de Pescado
8 tapas servings

In Spain one finds many variations of *buñuelos*, both as a savory and a sweet dish. It will be obvious from the simplicity of the following recipe that with a little imagination many alternatives are available.

1 lb/500 g potatoes, peeled and boiled
8 oz/250 g steamed cod, boned
1 garlic clove, finely chopped or pressed
1 tablespoon chopped parsley
pinch each of salt and pepper
4 egg yolks
oil for frying

1. Mash the potatoes thoroughly, without adding anything. Crumble the cod into the potatoes and then add the garlic, parsley, salt and pepper. Stir in the egg yolks last and mix thoroughly; it is important to get the mixture smooth.

2. In a pan heat about 1 ¼ in (3 cm) of oil until hot. Drop in about ½ tablespoon of the mixture at a time and fry the *buñuelos* until golden on all sides. Drain on paper towels. Serve hot.

FISH ROLLS
Rollo de Lenguado
6 tapas servings

¼ cup/2 oz/60 g butter
1 onion, finely chopped
3 oz/100 g shrimp (prawns), very finely chopped
1 tablespoon Spanish brandy
½ cup/2 oz/60 g fresh breadcrumbs
2 tablespoons fresh cream
1 tablespoon chopped parsley
1 egg, lightly beaten
6 fillets sole, cut in half lengthwise along the backbone
juice of 1 lemon
salt and freshly ground pepper

1. Preheat oven to 350°F/180°C/Gas 4. In a pan, fry the onion in half the butter until it is transparent. Add the shrimp and cook for 1 minute. Add the brandy and cook for a further minute, then add the breadcrumbs, cream and parsley and combine. Remove from heat and stir in the egg.

2. Place a portion of the mixture on each fillet, roll up and secure with a toothpick. Grease a small baking tray with the remaining butter. Place the rolled fish fillets in the tray, squeeze the lemon over them, then dust them with salt and pepper. Cover with aluminum foil and bake for 10 to 15 minutes. Serve immediately with the juices from the pan poured over the fish rolls.

BATTER-FRIED FISH
Pescado Frito
8 tapas servings

1 cup/8 fl oz/250 ml cold water
1 cup/4 oz/125 g all purpose (plain) flour
½ cup/2 oz/60 g cornstarch (cornflour)
pinch of salt
dash of lemon juice
1 egg yolk
1 lb/500 g bream or similar fish
oil for frying
flour for dredging

1. Whisk the cold water with the flour and cornstarch until completely smooth. (Dip your finger into the batter; it should run off, leaving just a thin coating on your finger.) Whisk in the salt, lemon juice and egg yolk. Refrigerate the batter for about 15 minutes.

2. Cut the fish into 2¼ × 1¼ in (6 × 3 cm) strips. Heat plenty of oil in a pan to around 400°F (200°C). Dredge the pieces of fish in flour and then coat with the batter. Fry until golden brown on both sides. Drain on paper towels and serve immediately.

BONED GARLIC SARDINES

Sardinas al Ajillo

about 10 tapas servings

1 lb/500 g fresh sardines
seasoned flour
3 oz/100 g garlic butter (page 60)
juice of 1 lemon

1. Clean and bone the sardines as described below.

2. Open the sardines out flat on a board and trim the edges. Dredge in the seasoned flour and arrange on a greased tray skin side down. Coat each sardine with garlic butter and sprinkle with lemon juice. Broil (grill) for 2 to 3 minutes under a preheated broiler (grill); do not overcook or they will dry out. Serve immediately.

Boning sardines: Cut off the head. Grip the tail between the thumb and forefinger of one hand, then free the backbone and pull it out with the other hand, leaving the tail intact.

STUFFED SARDINES
Sardinas Rellenos
6 tapas servings

2 tablespoons breadcrumbs
2 tablespoons olive oil
2 teaspoons finely chopped garlic
1 tablespoon chopped parsley
freshly ground black pepper
1 lb/500 g fresh sardines, cleaned and boned (page 89)
2 tablespoons lemon juice
parsley sprigs
lemon wedges
crusty bread

1. Preheat oven to 400°F/200°C/Gas 6. In a pan, fry the breadcrumbs in 1 tablespoon of the olive oil for 2 minutes. Add the garlic, parsley and black pepper and cook 1 minute.

2. Spoon a little of the mixture on to each flattened out sardine and then roll up from the head end so the tail is left on the outside.

3. Grease a baking dish with the remaining olive oil and pack the sardines together tails up. Pour the lemon juice over them and bake for 20 minutes. Serve immediately with the pan juices poured over the sardines. Garnish with parsley sprigs and lemon wedges and accompany with crusty bread that has been warmed in the oven.

SPICY MARINATED SARDINES
Sardinas en Escabeche Picante
15 to 20 tapas servings

This is a personal adaptation of the traditional Spanish method of preserving sardines; if you would prefer the traditional Spanish marinade, omit the ginger, *sambal oelek* and coriander and add a bunch each of fresh thyme and oregano with the vinegar.

2 ¼ lb/1 kg fresh sardines
flour for dredging, seasoned with salt and a little chili powder
Spanish olive oil for frying
Escabeche:
1 qt/1 l Spanish olive oil
20 whole unpeeled garlic cloves, smashed to break the skin
2 large onions, thinly sliced
1 tablespoon minced fresh ginger
1 tablespoon chopped coriander root
1 cup/8 fl oz/250 ml tomato puree
2 tablespoons tomato paste (concentrate)
3 cups/24 fl oz/750 ml red wine vinegar
12 bay leaves
1 to 2 tablespoons *sambal oelek* (page 115)
2 tablespoons chopped coriander (cilantro)
4 red bell peppers (capsicums), roasted, peeled, seeded and
cut into strips (page 19)

1. Clean sardines and cut off the heads. Wash and dry the fish, dredge in seasoned flour and shake off excess. Brown quickly in olive oil on both sides; do not cook through. Drain on paper towels.

2. For the *escabeche*, heat the olive oil in a nonaluminum pot until moderately hot. Add garlic cloves, onion, ginger and coriander root and cook 5 minutes. Stir in the tomato puree, tomato paste, vinegar, bay leaves, *sambal*, coriander and salt to taste, and simmer 30 minutes.

3. Meanwhile, layer the sardines compactly in an earthenware or stainless steel container, interspersing the layers with the red pepper strips. Pour the marinade over the sardines, making sure that all are well covered. Cool, cover and refrigerate at least 4 days before serving; until the bones soften completely. Serve chilled.

MARINATED SMELTS
Boquerones
8 tapas servings

Boquerones are another of the evergreens that are synonymous with tapas bars in Spain. Usually they are a small fish like a filleted smelt or unsalted anchovy. They are available in cans from continental delicatessens and I recommend that, rather than trying to work with the small fresh fish, you buy them and proceed from there.

1 lb/500 g can *boquerones*
¼ cup/2 fl oz/60 ml white wine vinegar
4 garlic cloves, minced
1 tablespoon chopped parsley

1. Discard the vinegar sauce from the can of *boquerones*. Wash the fish, then marinate them overnight in the refrigerator in the fresh vinegar, garlic and parsley.

2. Another version of *boquerones*, which is not traditionally Spanish but which I found very popular when I served it in Spain, was to drain the vinegar and then marinate the fish in a mixture of mild sour cream and a little chopped dill.

3. Serve cold in the marinade.

BASQUE-STYLE COD WITH GREEN PEAS
Merluza con Guisantes
10 tapas servings

This is a very popular dish from the Basque country in the north of Spain.

½ cup/4 fl oz/125 ml olive oil
20 small fillets of cod or similar fish
seasoned flour
juice of 1 lemon
½ cup/2 oz/60 g finely chopped onion
2 tablespoons flour
5 to 7 oz (150 to 200 g) can clams, juice reserved
1 cup/8 fl oz/250 ml white wine
6 garlic cloves, peeled
1 ½ cups/6 oz/180 g fresh or frozen green peas
½ cup/1 oz/30 g chopped parsley
salt and freshly ground pepper
2 hard-boiled eggs, finely chopped

1. Heat about half the olive oil in a large pan until smoking. Dust the fish in the seasoned flour and fry each piece for 30 to 60 seconds per side. Set aside in a casserole and pour the lemon juice over.

2. Heat the remaining olive oil in another pan and sauté the onion until transparent. Stir in the flour and cook for 1 minute. Gradually stir in the juice from the can of clams and the wine. Add the whole garlic cloves, peas, parsley and a little salt and pepper. Remove from heat and add the clams. Pour this mixture over the fish.

3. Preheat oven to 350°F/180°C/Gas 4. Bake the fish for 15 minutes. Sprinkle with the hard-boiled egg and serve.

TUNA IN VINAIGRETTE MARINADE
Escabeche de Atún
6 tapas servings

Many different types of fish are used for this dish, the most common being tuna, mackerel, trout and sardines. It is important to note that the fish should be lightly cooked, not overdone.

1 cup/8 fl oz/250 ml olive oil
½ cup/4 fl oz/125 ml red wine vinegar
½ cup/4 oz/125 ml finely chopped onion
1 teaspoon hot paprika or *sambal oelek* (page 115)
juice of ½ lemon
salt and freshly ground pepper
1 lb/500 g cooked tuna, cubed

Mix all the marinade ingredients thoroughly and pour over the fish. Cover and refrigerate for 24 to 48 hours before serving.

MARINATED RAW TUNA
Atún Crudo
8 tapas servings

8 oz/250 g yellowfin tuna or fresh snapper, bream, kingfish or
ocean trout
1 cup/8 fl oz/250 ml fresh lime juice
1½ cups/12 fl oz/375 ml canned unsweetened coconut milk
1 tablespoon chopped coriander (cilantro)
1 scant tablespoon seeded and finely sliced red chili
1 red onion, finely diced

1. Cut the fish into ⅓ in (1 cm) cubes. Place in a bowl with the lime
juice and marinate at least 4 hours, turning the pieces every so often
until they are thoroughly "bleached".

2. Pour off the lime juice. Add all remaining ingredients to the fish and
marinate for at least another hour. Serve cold.

MEATBALLS
Albóndigas
12 tapas servings

In Spain one would usually prepare this dish using ground (minced) pork, but beef is a perfectly good alternative. The following recipe will produce about 40 to 50 meatballs if you make them about 1 in (2.5 cm) in diameter. Serve the prepared meatballs in Simple Tomato Sauce (page 97).

1 lb/500 g ground pork or beef
½ cup/2 oz/60 g finely chopped onion
4 garlic cloves, finely chopped or pressed
1 tablespoon chopped parsley
½ cup/2 oz/60 g fine breadcrumbs
3 eggs
1 red chili, minced, or a dash of chili sauce
freshly ground black pepper
salt
flour for rolling

1. Combine all ingredients, mixing thoroughly. Let stand 30 minutes to allow the flavors to combine.

2. Roll the meatballs in flour. Deep fry in enough hot oil to cover, turning once, until cooked through. When served as a *tapa, albóndigas* are traditionally presented with garlic mayonnaise (page 114) as a dip, or reheated in a rich tomato sauce such as Simple Tomato Sauce.

SIMPLE TOMATO SAUCE
Yields 3 cups/24 fl oz/750 ml

This rich tomato sauce is the perfect accompaniment with *Albóndigas* (page 96).

1 onion, finely chopped
2 garlic cloves, finely chopped or pressed
olive oil
1 lb/465 g can Italian tomatoes, pureed
2 or 3 bay leaves
salt and freshly ground pepper
an aromatic herb such as thyme (optional)

Fry the onion and garlic in a little oil until transparent. Add the tomatoes, bay leaves, salt, pepper and herb and simmer 30 minutes on low to medium heat. If using this sauce as an accompaniment with *albóndigas*, add the meatballs now and keep hot by simmering in the sauce. If you are serving the meatballs in the sauce, garnish with parsley or chives.

Variation: For an alternative sauce, add 6 finely chopped garlic cloves and 1 tablespoon chopped parsley to ½ cup/4 oz/125 g melted butter. Simmer on low heat for 2 minutes to allow the flavors to combine. Do not overheat. Serve hot.

MOORISH-STYLE KEBABS
Pinchos Morunos
8 tapas servings

Since Spain was occupied by the Arabs for eight hundred years, one naturally finds many Moorish influences on its architecture, culture and food. This dish, which has remained popular in Spain throughout the centuries, is almost identical to one found in North Africa, with the notable exception that pork is generally used instead of lamb.

½ cup/4 fl oz/125 ml olive oil
1 teaspoon fresh thyme
1 teaspoon chili powder
1 teaspoon paprika
2 teaspoons ground cumin
1 teaspoon freshly ground pepper
1 teaspoon salt
1 ½ teaspoons chopped parsley
1 to 1 ½ lb (500 to 750 g) lean pork, cut into ¾ in (2 cm) cubes

1. Combine all ingredients except meat in a large bowl. Add the meat and stir to coat well. Cover and refrigerate overnight.

2. Thread the pieces of meat on skewers and cook over charcoal to desired doneness, basting frequently with the marinade. Serve at once.

PIGS' TROTTERS IN VINAIGRETTE SAUCE
Manos de Cerdo en Escabeche
12 tapas servings

This dish is normally served cold but is also delicious hot. To serve hot, place the pan in a preheated 350°F/180°C/Gas 4 oven for about 20 minutes or until the trotters are heated through.

6 pigs' trotters, split in half lengthwise
1 ham bone, or 2 bacon bones
1 medium onion, peeled and quartered
1 carrot
2 bay leaves
2 garlic cloves, peeled
6 black peppercorns
Escabeche:
1 cup/8 fl oz/250 ml olive oil
½ cup/4 fl oz/125 ml red wine vinegar
½ cup/2 oz/60 g finely chopped onion
1 teaspoon hot paprika
juice of ½ lemon
freshly ground pepper

1. Tie a length of string around each pig's trotter to keep them from falling apart. Place them in a pot along with the ham bone, onion, carrot, bay leaves, whole garlic cloves and peppercorns. Cover with water and bring to boil, tightly covered. Simmer for about 4 hours or until the trotters are extremely tender. Remove the trotters and carefully remove the string.

2. Mix the *escabeche* ingredients in a large, shallow nonaluminum pan. Place the trotters in this marinade and refrigerate overnight, turning several times.

SPANISH SAUSAGE, RED PEPPER (CAPSICUM) AND WINE
Chorizo, Pimiento y Vino
8 tapas servings

1 lb/500 g *chorizo*, thinly sliced
1 garlic clove, chopped
1 tablespoon chopped parsley
3 large red bell peppers (capsicums), roasted, peeled, seeded and sliced (page 19)
½ cup/4 fl oz/125 ml dry red wine

Preheat oven to 350°F/180°C/Gas 4. Fry the *chorizo* until browned; drain on paper towels. Arrange the *chorizo*, garlic, parsley and peppers in a baking dish and pour the wine over. Cover and bake for 10 minutes. Serve hot.

LAMB BROCHETTES WITH ROSEMARY
Pinchos de Cordero con Romero
10 tapas servings

To obtain the real flavor of this dish, the meat should be diced and marinated for 24 hours.

2 ¼ lb/1 kg boned loin of lamb
1 cup/2 oz/60 g chopped fresh rosemary
2 cloves garlic, finely chopped
juice of 2 lemons
salt and freshly ground black pepper
1 cup/8 fl oz/250 ml olive oil

1. Cut the lamb into 1 in (2.5 cm) dice. Mix together the rest of the ingredients and pour over the meat. Marinate lamb overnight.

2. Thread meat onto skewers and cook on the *plancha* (griddle) or on a barbecue, continually basting with the marinade. Serve at once.

LIVER WITH ONIONS
Hígado con Cebolla
8 tapas servings

1 lb/500 g calves' liver, thinly sliced
1 ½ teaspoons flour
olive oil
2 onions, finely chopped
salt and freshly ground pepper
1 teaspoon paprika
1 ½ teaspoons chopped fresh fennel
1 ½ teaspoons chopped parsley
⅔ cup/5 fl oz/150 ml dry red wine
1 teaspoon tomato paste (concentrate) dissolved in 1 cup/8 fl oz/250 ml water
1 red bell pepper (capsicum), roasted, peeled, seeded and cut into strips (page 19)

1. Dredge the liver in flour and brown quickly in olive oil. Remove from the pan and set aside, then fry the onions in the same oil until transparent. Stir in 1 ½ teaspoons flour, the salt, pepper, paprika, fennel and parsley and cook for 1 minute.

2. Add the wine and tomato mixture and stir to a good sauce consistency. Add the bell pepper and liver and cook for 4 to 5 minutes, making sure not to overcook the liver. Serve immediately.

LAMB'S LIVERS WITH BACON AND MUSTARD

Hígado con Tocino y Mostaza

8 tapas servings

The flour that is used to dredge the liver creates a nice, thick sauce. Browning the liver in two batches ensures even cooking. Don't overcook the liver or it will become dry.

1 large or 2 small lamb livers
4 tablespoons butter
2 onions, thinly sliced
seasoned flour for dredging
8 slices lean bacon
1 to 2 tablespoons prepared Hot English mustard to taste
2 tablespoons cognac
2 teaspoons freshly ground pepper
½ cup/2 oz/60 g chopped green (spring) onion tops

1. Remove the skin from the livers and slice the livers very thinly, discarding fat and gristle. Melt half the butter in a large pan. Add half the onion and sauté for 2 to 3 minutes. Dredge half the liver in seasoned flour, add to the pan and cook until well browned on the outside but still uncooked in the center. Remove from heat.

2. Repeat the process with the remaining butter, onion, flour and liver in a second pan.

3. Combine the contents of both pans. Broil (grill) the bacon and add it to the mixture with the mustard, cognac, pepper and onion tops. Return the pan to the heat, add about 1 cup/8 fl oz/250 ml water to make a thick sauce and cook only until the liver is cooked through.

LAMB'S LIVER MALLORCAN STYLE
Hígado Mallorquin
8 tapas servings

This is an adaptation of a Mallorcan favorite. The original, however, contains not only the liver but the lungs, heart and spleen of the sheep.

1 lamb's liver
1 cup/8 fl oz/250 ml olive oil
2 large potatoes, peeled and cut into ½ in (1 cm) dice
1 eggplant (aubergine), skin on, cut into ½ in (1 cm) dice
2 garlic cloves, coarsely chopped
1 red bell pepper (capsicum), cut into ½ in (1 cm) dice
1 large onion, finely chopped
2 dried red chilies, finely chopped
1 large red tomato, finely diced
2 tablespoons chopped fennel
salt and pepper
½ cup/4 fl oz/125 ml water

1. Skin and finely dice the lamb's liver, discarding the fat and sinew.

2. Heat the olive oil in a pan and fry the potato until it is almost cooked. Remove and let drain on paper towels. Brown the diced liver, then remove and drain on paper towels. Fry the eggplant with the garlic, remove and let drain on paper towels.

3. Fry the bell pepper, onion, and chili and cook until the onion is transparent. Add the tomato, fennel, salt and pepper and cook for 2 minutes. Add the water and return the other ingredients to the pan. Reduce the heat and simmer until the liver is cooked through and the sauce is reasonably dry, about 3 or 4 minutes. Serve hot.

TONGUE WITH CAPERS
Lengua con Alcaparras
6 tapas servings

1 sheep's tongue
1 tablespoon olive oil
½ cup/2 oz/60 g finely chopped onion
1 tablespoon flour
¾ cup/6 fl oz/175 ml white wine
1 tablespoon chopped parsley
salt and freshly ground pepper
2 tablespoons capers

1. Dip sheep's tongue in boiling water for 3 to 4 minutes. Douse in cold water then remove the skin and cut the tongue into ⅓ in (1 cm) slices.

2. Heat the olive oil in a pan and sauté the onion until transparent. Stir in the flour and cook for 1 minute. Add all remaining ingredients except the capers and simmer for 15 minutes or until the tongue is tender. Add the capers and serve.

KIDNEYS IN SHERRY SAUCE
Riñones al Jerez
8 tapas servings

If you reheat this dish, be careful not to overcook the kidneys as they will become dry and mealy.

2 veal or lambs' kidneys
2 tablespoons olive oil
1 onion, finely chopped
2 garlic cloves, finely chopped or pressed
1 ½ tablespoons chopped parsley
1 tablespoon flour
1 cup/8 fl oz/250 ml sherry
juice of 1 lemon
½ cup/4 fl oz/125 ml water
salt and freshly ground pepper

1. Remove skin, fat and membranes from the kidneys. Wash kidneys thoroughly and cut into ¼ in (0.5 cm) slices.*

2. Heat the olive oil in a pan and fry the kidney slices for about 1 ½ minutes or until browned on both sides. Remove and set aside on a paper towel. Sauté the onion, garlic and parsley in the same oil for 3 minutes. Add the flour and cook for 1 minute more, stirring well. Add the sherry, lemon juice and water and stir until smooth, then cook for 5 minutes. Add the kidneys and cook 2 more minutes. Serve immediately.

Note: If you wish, marinate the kidney slices in milk for an hour or two to rid them of their saltiness.

TRIPE
Callos

8 tapas servings

1 lb/500 g tripe
3 oz/100 g fresh or canned tomato
1 onion, quartered
16 garlic cloves, peeled
10 black peppercorns
2 whole cloves
2 bay leaves
2 sprigs parsley
pinch of aromatic herb such as thyme or oregano
1 ham bone or several bacon bones
olive oil
1 onion, finely chopped
½ cup/3 oz/90 g diced salt pork
1 *chorizo* sausage, diced
1½ teaspoons flour
1½ teaspoons paprika
5 oz/150 g canned peeled Italian tomatoes
2 chilies, seeded and chopped
½ cup/4 fl oz/60 ml white wine
chopped parsley

1. Wash the tripe thoroughly, then blanch it for 3 minutes in a large pot of boiling water. Drain and cut the tripe into ¾ in (2 cm) squares.

2. Cover the tripe with fresh water. Add the tomato, quartered onion, 8 garlic cloves, peppercorns, cloves, bay leaves, parsley sprigs, herb and bone and cook, covered, for about 4 hours or until the tripe is almost tender. Discard all but 2 cups/16 fl oz/500 ml of the cooking liquid.

3. Heat the olive oil in a pan and fry the chopped onion until transparent. Add the salt pork, *chorizo* and remaining garlic and cook for 2 minutes. Stir in the flour and paprika and cook for 2 minutes, then add the canned tomatoes, chilies, wine and 1 cup/8 fl oz/250 ml of the tripe cooking liquid. Cook, covered, for 15 minutes.

4. Add the tripe, uncover and cook for a further hour; if the sauce is reducing too much, add more reserved cooking liquid as needed. Sprinkle with parsley and serve.

CHICKEN LEGS
Piernas de Pollo
8 tapas servings

16 chicken legs, skin removed
flour for dredging
olive oil for frying
1 onion, finely chopped
1 tablespoon chopped garlic
1 lb/465 g can Italian whole peeled tomatoes
1 cup/8 fl oz/250 ml chicken stock
salt and freshly ground black pepper

1. Preheat oven to 300°F/150°C/Gas 2. Dredge the chicken legs in flour and fry them in the olive oil until they are evenly browned. Remove chicken from pan and retain some oil to sauté the onion and garlic until the onion is transparent. Add the tomatoes and cook for 15 minutes. Remove from the heat and puree in a blender or food processor with the chicken stock. Season with salt and pepper.

2. Arrange the chicken legs in a baking tray and cover with the tomato sauce. Cover with foil and bake for 1 hour. Remove the foil, turn the chicken in the sauce, pour off any excess liquid and bake for a further 30 minutes. (The chicken will be beautifully tender.) Serve immediately.

CHICKEN SALAD
Ensalada de Pollo

12 tapas servings

2 ¼ to 3 ¼ lb/1 to 1.5 kg whole roast chicken
4 sticks celery, finely diced
1 apple, peeled and diced
2 red bell peppers (capsicums), seeds and inner membrane
removed, finely diced
1 cucumber, skinned, seeded and finely diced
1 pear, peeled and diced
10 green (spring) onions, green tops only, finely chopped
1 cup/8 fl oz/250 ml mayonnaise (page 114)
salt and freshly ground pepper

Remove meat from the chicken and cut into 1 in (2.5 cm) dice. Combine
with all the other ingredients and allow to stand in the refrigerator for
30 minutes before serving.

QUAIL IN COGNAC SAUCE
Codornices en Salsa de Coñac
8 tapas servings

Served individually, the quail are an ideal snack size. If you want to make a main course out of this dish, serve two quail per person with vegetables.

½ cup/4 fl oz/125 ml olive oil
8 strips lean bacon
8 quail
1 cup/4 oz/125 g onion, finely chopped
3 garlic cloves, finely chopped or pressed
½ cup/4 fl oz/125 ml Spanish brandy or cognac
2 tablespoons chopped parsley
1 bay leaf
pinch of thyme
freshly ground pepper

1. Heat the oil in a pan large enough to hold all the quail. Tie a strip of bacon around each bird and fry them until the bacon is completely cooked and the quail are browning.

2. Pour off half the oil. Add the onion and garlic and fry for 2 to 3 minutes. Add the brandy and ignite, shaking the pan gently until the flames subside. Add all remaining ingredients, cover and cook over medium heat until the quail are cooked through and tender, about 10 minutes.

EMPANADA PASTRY
Empanada
Makes enough for 60 empanadas

The filled pastries known as empanadas come in many varieties. Not only are they common in Spain but they can also be found in the southwestern states of the United States as well as throughout Central and South America. The secret of getting empanadas right is in having the filling mixture at the right consistency and the pastry at the right temperature.

A good filling should be reasonably thick, with no oil or liquids exuding from it. (This makes it difficult to join the pastry edges together.) The filling should be cold when you fill the pastry so that it doesn't soften the dough. It's best to keep the pastry circles in the refrigerator, removing and filling only four or five at a time.

This recipe makes a pastry that is lighter than the traditional Spanish one, but I have found that most people prefer it.

9 cups/2¼ lb/1 kg all purpose (plain) flour
2 cups/16 fl oz/500 ml cold water, approximately
generous pinch of salt
1 lb/500 g butter, room temperature

1. Pile the flour on a pastry board and make a well in the center. Gradually mix in enough water to make a smooth, workable dough, adding the salt at some point during this process. Knead the dough for at least 7 to 8 minutes, continually turning and folding it back onto itself. Wrap the dough in plastic wrap and let rest in the refrigerator for at least 30 minutes.

2. On a floured board, roll the dough out into a large, thin sheet. Spread the butter (which should be room temperature soft, but not melting) evenly over the dough. Fold the edges into the center at least four times. Wrap and return it to the refrigerator for 30 minutes.

3. Again roll the dough out on the floured board and fold it over at least eight times. Return to the refrigerator for another 30 minutes, then roll the dough to ¹⁄₁₆ in (2 mm) thick and cut into 4 in (10 cm) circles, pressing together and rerolling the scraps. Lightly flour the circles and return them to the refrigerator for 30 minutes. Bring them out four or five at a time to fill them.

EMPANADA PASTRY

4. Place 1 to 2 teaspoons of filling mixture in the center of each pastry circle; fold in half and crimp the edges together. Pinch the edge between your thumb and forefinger and turn inward; this will ensure that no filling leaks out.

5. If you cannot be bothered going through the process of making your own pastry (which produces an admirably better result), empanada pastry is available in Spanish and South American delicatessens or you can use a commercial puff or short pastry. The type that comes in rolled sheets is already the approximate thickness required for empanadas. After you have cut out the circles, let them rest in the refrigerator for at least 30 minutes and take out just a few at a time as described above.

GLOSSARY

The ingredients in this book are generally easy to find. Spanish olives, olive oil and wines have become popular over the past few years. There are only a handful of items that you may find harder to track down, and these are listed here along with advice about the use of some more familiar ones.

Aguardiente A very strong Spanish liqueur similar in type to Italian grappa which can be used as a substitute. It gives a distinctive flavor to cooking but should be used in moderation.

Blood sausage Available from most delicatessens, blood sausage is made with diced pork or pork fat, beef blood and spices. It is very dark in appearance.

Chili peppers Red chilies are frequently used in Spanish tapas. They are more often used in their dried form and are to add a tang to a dish rather than to make it spicy-hot. Having given this advice you will note that I completely ignore it myself and tend to be heavy-handed with chili in quite a few recipes. This is a personal preference and one that has always seemed to meet with the approval of those sampling the dishes. Rather than using dried or fresh chilies, I usually add them in the form of **sambal oelek**, which is an Indonesian chili sauce containing red chilies, salt and vinegar. I find the best way to keep chili on hand is simply to have a jar of *sambal* in the refrigerator. It keeps for ages, has a great flavor and is available from Asian shops and many delicatessens.

Chorizo *Chorizo* is a Spanish pork sausage that has an orange tint due to the presence of paprika. It has many uses in cooking, and is often sliced and eaten cold or fried and served with bread. *Chorizo* and other Spanish sausages are available at Spanish, Portuguese or South American delicatessens.

Clams Small clams are not so easy to find. If you can't get hold of the smaller ones, use the larger variety and reduce the suggested quantities in the recipes. But a word of warning: the larger clams are tougher.

Cognac I have specified cognac in several recipes. If you can find good Spanish brandy it is the preferred ingredient, but if not use a French cognac or brandy. Don't try to get away with using a cheap brandy, as it can mar the flavor of a dish like Quail in Cognac Sauce.

Mayonnaise and Garlic Mayonnaise (Mayonesa y Alïoli) Both mayonnaise and garlic mayonnaise are common ingredients in and accompaniments to tapas. While both are available in prepared form, you will achieve infinitely better results by preparing your own according to the Spanish recipe. Both regular and garlic mayonnaise will keep in the refrigerator for at least a week, tightly covered. This recipe yields 3 cups/24 fl oz/750 ml.

3 egg yolks
1 tablespoon white wine vinegar
salt and pepper
pinch of sugar
2 cups/16 fl oz/500 ml olive oil
1 teaspoon lemon juice

Combine the egg yolks, vinegar, mustard, sugar, salt and pepper in a large bowl and whisk to blend. Very slowly whisk in the olive oil a few drops at a time, gradually increasing to a very slow stream as the mixture emulsifies. Mix in the lemon juice last. Check the flavor and adjust if necessary.

To make in a food processor, use the plastic blade. Start with the egg yolks and pour the olive oil in a little at a time. When the mixture begins to emulsify and thicken, alternate the other ingredients with the olive oil until it is all used. Check the flavor and adjust if necessary.

Should the mixture separate (which usually occurs by adding the oil too quickly) stop immediately, tip the mixture into a bowl, add 2 fresh egg yolks and start again with remainig ingredients. Lastly, very slow and carefully add the separated mix to the new mix.

For Garlic Mayonnaise: add 2 or more minced garlic cloves to the egg yolk mixture.

Octopus If you cannot obtain tenderized baby octopus or if you have a ready supply of larger fresh octopus, follow the procedure below.

Holding the octopus firmly, beat or throw it forcefully against a hard surface (such as concrete) about 30 or 40 times. Clean each octopus thoroughly and discard the head. Remove the little hard ball, or "beak", in the center of the octopus and cut off the last ¾ in (2 cm) of the tentacles.

Half-fill a pot large enough to accommodate the octopus with water and bring it to boil. Immerse the octopus in the boiling water for 30 seconds, then remove it. Bring the water back to the boil and repeat the process three more times. Bring the water to boil again and add, for each 2 quarts/2 liters of water, a peeled onion studded with 6 cloves, 1 bay leaf, 6 white peppercorns and 2 tablespoons vinegar. Add the octopus and simmer gently. There is no exact formula as to how long to cook the octopus; it will depend on how successful you have been in tenderizing it and on the thickness of the tentacles. After one hour, remove a piece of octopus and bite into it to test for tenderness; repeat this process every 15 minutes or so until the octopus is tender. (Cooking can take one hour or as long as three.) Drain the cooked octopus and cut the tentacles into bite-size cross-sections.

In Spain the recipes for *Pulpo a la Gallega* (page 84) and *Pulpo en Escabeche* (page 85) usually employ octopus cooked in this manner.

GLOSSARY

Olive oil   Where olive oil is specified it is important to use Spanish olive oil. It is readily available and has a distinct flavor that is essential to many of these recipes.

Sambal oelek   See chili peppers (page 113).

Squid (Calamar)   Pay a little extra and buy small, fresh squid rather than the frozen tubes. You have to go to the bother of cleaning them out, but the reward is in infinitely better flavor.

Serrano   *Serrano* and *jamón serrano* are best-quality hams from the mountain regions of Spain. Proscuitto (Italian ham) is an adequate substitute.

Tocino   *Tocino* is a type of cured pork similar to bacon, yet with a subtly different flavor. It is often sold in Mediterranean-style delicatessens, but if it is not available use pancetta or bacon.

Tomatoes   Where tasty, vine-ripened tomatoes are unavailable I always use the canned Italian variety. They give a far superior flavor.

INDEX

INDEX